# GROWING TOGETHER:

## Mother & Child

**LENORE BUTH**

# GROWING TOGETHER:

# Mother & Child

LENORE BUTH

CONCORDIA®
Publishing House
St. Louis

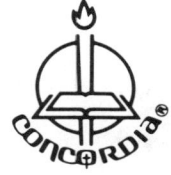

Hypothetical situations are used as illustrations in this book; in such instances all names are fictional.

Unless otherwise indicated, Scripture quotations are from The Holy Bible: NEW INTERNATIONAL VERSION. Copyright © 1978 by the International Bible Society. Used by permission of Zondervan Bible Publishers.

Biblical references marked RSV are from the Revised Standard Version of the Bible, copyrighted 1946, 1952 © 1971, 1973. Used by permission.

Verses marked TLB are taken from THE LIVING BIBLE, © 1971 by Tyndale House Publishers, Wheaton, Illinois. Used by permission.

Unless otherwise indicated, most quotations used at the beginning of chapters are from one of the following:
*Living Quotations for Christians*, edited by Sherwood Eliot Wirt and Kersten Beckstrom. Harper & Row, 1974.
*The Encyclopedia of Religious Quotations*, edited by Frank S. Mead. Revell, 1976.
*Peter's Quotations—Ideas for Our Time*, by Dr. Laurence J. Peter. Bantam Books, 1977.
*Say It Again*, collected by Dorothy Uris. Dutton, 1979.
*Dictionary of Quotations*, collected by Bergen Evans. Delacorte Press, 1968.

Copyright © 1985 Concordia Publishing House
3558 South Jefferson Ave., St. Louis, MO 63118
Manufactured in the United States of America

All rights reserved. No part of this publication may be reproduced, stored in a retrieval system, or transmitted, in any form or by any means, electronic, mechanical, photocopying, recording, or otherwise, without the prior written permission of Concordia Publishing House.

---

Library of Congress Cataloging in Publication Data

Buth, Lenore.
    Growing together.

    (Friends for life)
    1. Mother and child. 2. Parenting—Religious aspects—Christianity. I. Title. II. Series: Friends for life (St. Louis, Missouri)
HQ759.B83 1985        306.8'743        84-23912
ISBN 0-570-03963-0

---

1 2 3 4 5 6 7 8 9 10   MAL   94 93 92 91 90 89 88 87 86 85

*To
Bev, Donna, Robbie, and Janet—
each special,
each my much-loved daughter,
each my very good friend.
And to Bob,
without whose love and support
neither children nor book would have come to be.*

# *Contents*

| | |
|---|---|
| Introduction | 9 |
| **1** Mothering Mother: If You Don't, Nobody Else Will! | 13 |
| **2** Of Birthing and Bonding: The Vital Preschool Years | 27 |
| **3** Mother or Chauffeur? Keeping Up with the Grade-Schooler | 42 |
| **4** "Really, Mother!" The Wonderful, Baffling Adolescent | 61 |
| **5** Nurturing and Nourishing in Special Situations: The Single Mother, the Stepmother, the Adoptive Mother | 86 |
| **6** Strengthening the Ties That Bind—While Cutting Them: The Young Adult | 104 |
| **7** They Keep Coming Back Like a Song: The Drop-in, Drop-out Adult Child | 116 |
| **8** Keeping a Good Thing Going—for Life! | 124 |
| Epilog | 138 |

# *Introduction*

*Train up a child in the way he should go,
and when he is old he will not depart from it.*
Prov. 22:6 RSV

Every Christian parent knows these familiar words. We have, in fact, had them drummed into our unconscious at every turn. And no wonder, for the truth of them is undeniable.

This same principle applies to the mother-child relationship, for like Rome, you can't build it in a day. The best time to lay the foundation for the close, comfortable, communicative bond you'll yearn for with your teenager is every day of every year from that child's birth.

Then, when your child reaches the teen years, talking things through and sharing feelings will already be a habit. And when your child becomes an adult, it will be natural to be accepting and honest with each other, because you always have been.

As you leaf through this book, be aware that the chapters are interrelated, as is childrearing. It's a step-by-step approach—each chapter builds on the preceding one. Reading the table of contents, you may wonder, "Where were you when I needed you?" Right now you may be parenting one or more exciting, challenging (and often maddening) teenagers. So why should you care about birthing and bonding and preschoolers?

There are at least two good reasons:

1. Principles of good parenting are timeless. You'll find that what helps cement the mother-child bond with toddlers, for instance, still proves to be good "glue" with teenage offspring.

2. You probably know at least one young mother whose own

mother is many miles away. This fledgling mom would probably love to have an experienced guide and friend—like you. Remember Titus 2:3-4? "Likewise, teach the older women to be reverent in the way they live . . . to teach what is good. Then they can train the younger women to love their husbands and children."

If your children are past infancy, you're an "older woman," at least in experience. God calls each of us to be an information source, an affirmer, a support to each other—but especially to the timid first-timers. So you'll want to know what today's crop of new mothers is reading and hearing. Then you can reassure your friend of the principles you've found to be true from your own experience.

There's one caution: As you read this (and other) books, you may think back on your years of child rearing and become burdened with guilt because of your fumbles and failures. Logic tells you that you were young and learning on the job, that you did the best you could at the time. Yet the nagging thought persists: did your blunders and omissions scar your children for life?

Or perhaps you feel discouraged because your home atmosphere is strained—a house full of strangers, almost, with little communication. Perhaps you've seen this distancing become a pattern, one that troubles you deeply. Yet you don't seem able to change yourself, let alone your family members.

Wherever you are right now, whatever your insufficiencies of the past or the present, don't despair. Rather, let's you and I go back to God's Word for our reassurance: "And we know that in all things God works for the good of those who love him, who have been called according to his purpose" (Rom. 8:28).

In *all* things! Our merciful, loving Father will take our humanly bungled job of parenting and fashion even our mistakes into good in the lives of our children. (Have we asked Him to do just that?) For our children are really just on loan to us from Him. Surely He wants their good even more than we!

So, having repented and been forgiven, forgive yourself and start from where you are now. You *can* begin anew! It's not too late to start restructuring and nurturing your mother-child relationship. (Remember the prodigal son and his father?) You'll need a bit more than usual of persistence and insight and sensitivity. You'll need a lot of love and an ample supply of patience. But it can be done. The God of renewal will be your enabler. Remember, you can do all things through Christ who strengthens you (Phil. 4:13). Confess your faults and inadequacies. Ask for His Holy Spirit's wisdom and guidance and healing and then *depend* on Him to be faithful to His promises.

Is it ever easy? No. The parent-child relationship is an edifice that's everlastingly under construction.

Is it worth the effort? Definitely!

The reward is the prize of parenting. You and your daughter or son can be not only mother and child but friends who truly enjoy each other's company—for a lifetime.

How do you forge this uncommon bond? Let us count the ways . . .

# 1

# Mothering Mother

## If You Don't, Nobody Else Will!

*Trust in the Lord with all your heart
    and lean not on your own understanding;
in all your ways acknowledge him,
    and he will make your paths straight.
. . . pay attention to what I say;
    listen closely to my words.
Do not let them out of your sight,
    keep them within your heart;
for they are life to those who find them
    and health to [the] whole body.
Above all else, guard your heart,
    for it is the wellspring of life.
Put away perversity from your mouth;
    keep corrupt talk far from your lips.
[She] who fears the Lord has a secure fortress,
    and for [her] children it will be a refuge.
Her children arise and call her blessed;
    her husband also, and he praises her . . .
Charm is deceptive, and beauty is fleeting;
    but a woman who fears the Lord is to be praised.
        Prov. 3:5-6; 4:20-24; 14:26; 31:28-30*

Probably most mothers from every sort of background would agree: being a mother is the most satisfying vocation of all. But it's also the most challenging, the most demanding, and surely the most exhausting!

Perhaps that's because you're on call 24 hours a day. Perhaps it's because you feel such total responsibility for your child's care and for shaping this precious bit of humanity for the future. Perhaps it's because you feel you must be everything you were before *and* a mother, besides.

Whatever. The point is that nothing quite prepares you for your task. And nothing quite prepares you for the feeling of being constantly drained as you seek to be all things to all people.

"Nobody ever told me it would be easy," says Angie, "but I didn't expect to feel overwhelmed 90 percent of the time—and tired down to my bones *all* the time! I'm constantly giving out, but I never have time—or energy—to put anything back in. I'm like a pitcher that's had everything inside it poured out . . . I often feel I have nothing left to give."

Her eyes fill with tears as she continues, this young mother of a six-month-old boy, a daughter who's in the "terrible twos," and another in kindergarten. "It tears me up inside because I'm not the kind of mother I want to be. Most of the time I just flounder along from day to day, doing the best I can but never quite catching up. Over and over again I resolve to try harder—and I fail. Then I get more uptight than ever. What's wrong with me? I just can't seem to get my act together!"

Probably the mother hasn't yet drawn breath who feels she's fully meeting each family member's needs or staying current with each task on her "to do" list. The secret of surviving motherhood, of not only coping but of finding strength for each day and deep joy as you watch your children grow, lies in this: develop your personal inner resources, for you can only give out what you have inside.

Mothering requires vitality, resilience, toughness—of spirit, body, and mind. You need a calm, solid core that remains unperturbed. For more than anyone or anything else, *you* are the human foundation on which your family rests.

But how do you maintain that serene center in the midst of crying children and dirty diapers, of temper tantrums and orthodontia, of Sesame Street and sibling spats and soccer practice?

There's only one way—by putting first things first. The model for all human bonds is seen in Christ's relationship with His Father. Our own most important relationship is with that same heavenly Father, through faith in Jesus Christ and by the witness of the Holy Spirit. That's the faithful foundation on which we build our mother-child relationship, and so we start there. The first thing—the *one* thing—that will give us enduring inner peace is to make nurturing our faith first priority for the day. Close behind it comes developing our physical and emotional strength.

"Well, I think that sounds very nice—and one of these days I will get into a good routine," says Angie. "But right now I don't even have time to think! The baby's crying before I get my eyes open in the morning. By the time I get the kids off to bed, I'm exhausted, and I just collapse. I don't have the energy to exercise—and I sure don't have an extra minute for Bible study. As for my emotions, well, I get depressed sometimes . . . but doesn't everybody?"

It's easy to be so swamped by the daily demands that we treat ourselves shabbily. Motherhood demands all that we have—and more! Changing roles notwithstanding, Mother is the center, the hub around which the wheel of the family revolves. When we're off-center, out-of-balance, the wheel won't function as smoothly. So taking care of ourselves (even if our preferred standards of housekeeping and cooking have to go) is not self-indulgence. Rather it's equipping ourselves for loving service to our families. It's faithful Christian stewardship of the being God created so that we can share the best of ourselves with those who matter most. It's preparation for the task that God has given us.

### *Physical Vitality*

*L*et's start with our bodies. You can find shelves of books in any library or bookstore that will give you basic principles of sound diet. Briefly stated, don't skip meals. Since most of us must count calories, be sure that you spend yours wisely. Concentrate on nourishing food rather than on "empty-calorie" snacks. Cut down on caffeine and sweets and eat plenty of vegetables and fruits. You need a balanced diet to be a balanced, energetic mother.

As for exercise, yes, you do cover lots of ground, and you're probably frazzled at the end of the day. Yet strangely enough, regular vigorous exercise—jogging, walking, aerobics, etc.—increases one's energy level. You may drag yourself, groaning, to exercise, but you'll have more pep and stamina as a result. Exercise is also an excellent way to lower stress levels. Be sure to work into any exercise program gradually and to have a medical checkup before beginning.

Can't leave your preschoolers alone? Can't afford a health club? Trade off time with a neighbor or friend and watch each other's children. Then each of you will have time to exercise. Some mothers get up and run before their husbands leave for work. (They find that their added energy makes up for lost sleep.) Others wait until Dad gets home from work, leaving a snack of carrot sticks or apple slices to prevent mutiny by the troops. As a bonus, this time can become a very special father-child occasion, too.

Getting enough rest is also vital. Often that "draggy" or depressed state of mind can be traced to long-accumulated fatigue. Have your doctor check out symptoms of ill health, of course. But try giving up that last hour of TV and going to bed instead. Whenever you get the children down for a nap, shut your eyes to the household clutter and take one yourself. You may be surprised to find out how your view of your world improves and how your liveliness increases. (Remember the contrast between how you felt before and after the baby started sleeping all night?)

Be aware, too, that your physical health is influenced by attitudes. When you're happy and contented, you truly *feel* better. When you think health, you're actually less likely to become ill.

## *Emotional Health*

**B**e selective about what you put in your mind—what you read, listen to, and watch. There's a slogan in computer language: GIGO. That stands for Garbage In—Garbage Out. The same is true of our mental computers.

So it's wise to practice thought control. When you find yourself feeling negative or resentful or sorry for yourself, *stop* right then before you get caught in the downward spiral. Bundle up the kids and go for a walk. Build a snowman. Go to the library. But do something different to break the cycle. That's all part of developing a positive attitude.

As Christians we know we have much for which to thank God. We're forgiven and washed clean by Jesus Christ's death and resurrection. That alone should make us joyful! And yet . . . we all have "down" days because we remain human beings. So along with asking the Lord to give us a joyful attitude, we need to do our part—to practice looking, as Grandma used to say, on the bright side of things.

We need positive action, too. Each of us needs at least one interest outside our family, something that we personally enjoy, though perhaps no other family member finds it appealing. It doesn't much matter what it is. Anna bought a bird book and likes nothing better than to tramp through the countryside with her binoculars. Marianne is a zoo volunteer and loves introducing youngsters to the baby animals in the petting zoo. Kathy reads to preschoolers during the weekly story time at her local library. Maggie is having the time of her life at an adult education painting class. Sarah enrolled in a community college history class and discovered that her new knowledge enriches her conversation and her understanding of the news. Debbie wished for a young mother's fellowship at her church, so she helped to start one and then volunteered to lead the Bible study. Doreen teamed up with another young mother, alternating babysitting and driving, so that they can deliver Meals on Wheels.

Your options are endless, no matter what your situation. Just find something that nurtures you and stimulates you. If your choice produces a nice warm glow inside, it's doing the trick.

Another key factor in emotional health is to know and accept yourself. Most people wear a mask, living up to an image they want to project, either for themselves or for someone else. But mask-wearing gets to be a dreadful strain, and it gets in the way of relationships—with people and with God, who sees through all our pretenses. Even though it takes time, even though it may sting, start peeling off the layers and looking deep within yourself. Start by asking the Holy Spirit to reveal you to yourself.

Chances are that some of the feelings that come to light won't make you proud. (Welcome to the club!) You may uncover fears and failures you'd long repressed; sin and shame that make you blush; memories that still have the power to make you weep. Yet, until you recognize and confront your feelings, how can you resolve them and thus be free of them?

If you're married, it's important to cultivate the love you share with your husband, too. *Make* time for just the two of you. Take weekend trips together, even if it's just to a downtown motel, and leave your children in the care of others. The stronger your marriage, the stronger your family will be. When your youngsters know that Mom and Dad love each other deeply, they feel more secure, more at peace. Your mutual love overflows to your offspring so that no matter what happens outside the home they (and you) know that all is well within.

## *Spiritual Well-Being*

*E*motional health is closely linked to spiritual health because there's only one way to leave that load of regret and self-recrimination behind, once and for all, and that's to lay everything at the feet of Jesus.

Simply tell Him honestly what you're feeling. Ask Him to take away what troubles you and to blot out even the memory of it. Share with Him what you'd like to be, like to feel. Tell your Savior that you're ready—if you are—to let His Spirit make you into the person He would have you to be. Ask for the Holy Spirit's peace and joy. (This is seldom a once-for-all process, because we're always changing and growing.)

The Good News of the Gospel is that God accepts us as we are now, not when we become what we (and He) want us to be (Rom. 5:8-10). So we can accept ourselves, too. You are a child of God, created to be a unique individual (Ps. 139:13-16). You are a sinful human being, true, but a redeemed human being, washed clean by the blood of Jesus Christ. "In him we have redemption through his blood, the forgiveness of sins, in accordance with the riches of God's grace" (Eph. 1:7).

Assured of God's forgiveness and peace, you need not wallow in guilt. Ask God to plant that assurance in your heart and mind so that you'll be solid spiritually. Then ask Him to give you His kind of acceptance of your children—that they, too, are okay as they are. Begin there, for your own faith and your self-acceptance form the basis for everything else you do and are as a mother.

## You Are the Key

*D*oes that sound like too strong a statement? Ask yourself: What kind of shape am I in spiritually? What's the state of the faith in my home?

Most likely whatever you answered to the first question will be echoed in your reply to the second. We may wish it weren't so, but we mothers are a major factor in the climate of faith in our homes. Indeed, our faith in God is meant to be a spontaneous, everyday part of the way we parents relate to our children:

> . . . love the Lord your God . . . serve him with all your heart and with all your soul. Fix these words of mine in your hearts and minds; tie them as symbols on your hands and bind them on your foreheads. Teach them to your children, talking about them when you sit at home and when you walk along the road, when you lie down and when you get up (Deut. 11:13, 18-19).

Paul's helper Timothy was reminded that his faith came to him as a child through his grandmother Lois and his mother, Eunice.

If we're to teach and to talk in a natural way, we need to store up the truth of God's Word in our hearts and minds. As with a bank account we can only draw out what we've previously deposited. In this day of instant everything, there's still only one way to accomplish this: make Bible reading and prayer a priority of daily life.

"That's what they always say!" exclaims Angie, impatiently, "but nobody ever tells me where I'm supposed to find the time!"

"Somehow we always have the time for what we consider important," says Carrie, gently. "I always managed to watch my favorite

TV soap operas and read the daily newspaper. Even read a lot of romance novels . . . But I never had the time to read the Bible, though I kept making good resolutions.

"I must have started and stopped a hundred times—but usually I only lasted a day or two," continues Carrie with a smile. "I finally found that the only way to avoid being sidetracked is to get up before Dave and the kids. Now I wouldn't miss it! Somehow that time with the Lord more than makes up for the sleep I miss. I like setting my focus right and laying my day before the Lord. Something else . . . I've found that the more hectic I expect the day to be, the more I need to get centered in the Lord. I don't s'pose it will ever be easy to pry my eyes open in the morning, but it sure is worth it!"

It is, of course, important for our own spiritual growth and that of our children to worship as a family within our own church and to attend Sunday school and Bible class (Ps. 29:2; 95:6-7; Luke 4:8; Heb. 10:25). In fact, many people feel that they can get by perfectly well with regular church attendance alone. Yet, if you asked whether it's possible to nourish a husband-wife relationship, for example, with just an hour or two of attention per week, you'd likely hear, "Don't be ridiculous!" as the answer.

## *Someone Is Watching You*

*I*t's imperative that our faith be well rooted and strong and growing, for the much-quoted maxim proves reliable: More is caught than taught.

True, faith is the work and the gift of God's Holy Spirit. But we're to model for our children what it means to be in a close relationship with Jesus Christ. That means that we *live* it day in and day out, not just talk about it. We mothers are to be attractive, authentic demonstrations of the Christian faith lived out in the nowhere-to-hide arena of the family.

It's sobering to realize that what we are, our children will likely become, for you and I painfully perceive our own faults. The Good News for us as Christian mothers is that God can build on the imperfect foundation we lay and that He will equip us for the challenges of our days, just as He promised to enable Timothy for his ministry:

*But as for you, continue in what you have learned and have firmly believed, knowing from whom you learned it and how from childhood you have been acquainted with the sacred writings which are able to instruct you for salvation through faith in Christ Jesus. All Scripture is inspired by God and profitable for teaching, for reproof, for correction and for training in righteousness, that the [person] of God may be complete, equipped for every good work (2 Tim. 3:14-17 RSV).*

To be complete, able not only to get through the day but to cope in confidence, to triumph *over* circumstances, isn't that what we all long for? On our own we cannot do it. But God is fully able and ready to work mature faith in us. As we offer our time and ourselves in reading His Word and talking with Him in prayer our "cope ability" grows.

## *One Way to Read and Pray*

You'll be glad to know that you needn't embark on an exhaustive analysis of the Bible, complete with commentary and study guide. Here's a simple method which can yield great spiritual growth:
- Use one of the newer translations for easier comprehension. There are a number available—the New International Version and Today's English Version, to name two.
- If you're new to Bible study, you might want to begin with the gospel of John. Later read some of Paul's epistles (letters)—Romans, Corinthians, Ephesians, etc.
- Begin by asking God's Holy Spirit to make you teachable and to reveal His truth in your heart.
- Read a few verses. Read until you get to a place that makes you want to stop and think about it.
- Mentally summarize what you've read. If you're unsure of or can't recall what you've read, go back and reread the passage. Ask yourself, "What is there in this Scripture that I can use in my life? Is there a challenge? Is there comfort? Is there something I need to change?" Take a few minutes and contemplate what you've read. Be open to the Holy Spirit's guidance.

- As you go through your day, think some more about what you read. Do you have any new ideas, new insights? Ask yourself, "How do I see God's hand in my life today?"
- When you find verses that seem especially helpful, underline them in your Bible. Deposit them in your "memory bank" so that they're ready for instant withdrawal whenever you need a lift from God's Word.
- The point is not how much of the Bible you read each day. The point is to get centered, anchored solidly in the truth of God's Word.

Perhaps you're thinking, "But the Bible is so hard to understand! Why can't I just substitute good Christian books?"

Simple. Any book, including this one, is a human being's pre-digested concepts. No matter who wrote it, no matter how widely acclaimed it is, there's no comparison between any other book and God's book. The Bible is our authority, the source book of our faith and our strength (Rom. 10:17; Col. 3:16; 1 Peter 1:23-25). Ask God's Holy Spirit to be your Teacher, to open the Word for you (1 Cor. 2:9-13).

Prayer is simply talking to your Father who loves you, as a child talks to his or her daddy.

- Begin by praising the Lord for what He *is*:

    "I praise You, Lord, because You are merciful, because You are faithful, because You are Lord of heaven and earth," and so forth.

    (You may want to just be silent for awhile and consider the greatness of God.) The Psalms can be a wonderful beginning for our praise. For instance, you could start by reading and pondering Psalm 8.

- Next thank Him for what He has done in your life:

    "I thank You, Lord, that You sent Your Son, Jesus Christ, to be my Savior from sin; I thank You for my health; I thank You for the children You've given me and for giving me strength to care for them, . . ."

- Confess your known sin:

    "Gracious Lord, I can't even meet my own standards. I have failed You in so many ways, including _____. By Your

Holy Spirit, would You open my heart and show me the sin that comes between us? (Pause for a brief moment of silence.) I bring my sin and my inadequacy before You. Cleanse me, make me whole, and empower me to be more like Jesus Christ, my Savior.

- Now bring your requests before Him:

  "Lord, please provide for our needs this day; bring healing in my disagreement with my neighbor; show me how to be more patient with my children; guide me to the right decision, . . ."

- Close by acknowledging that you're His child and want His will and that you ask in the name of your Savior:

  "Father, I leave these petitions in Your hand and trust You to work for my good. Most of all I want Your will in my life. I ask in the name of Jesus Christ, and I thank You because You have promised to hear us. Amen."

- If you find it hard to express yourself, you might pray through one or more of the Psalms. Many, like Psalm 16, are already written in the first person. For one like Psalm 20, substitute "me" for "you." You'll soon find favorites to fit whatever your emotions and needs may be at a given time.

These are general guidelines—don't get hung up on procedures and phrases, these or any others. Perhaps this sounds "too heavy," and you're not ready for it. That's okay. Begin with what you feel most comfortable and choose a time that suits your schedule. Just begin.

You won't have a perfect record—a mother's life is not predictable! But make it your goal to take in the real "soul food" every day. Your spirit needs frequent nourishment if you're to be strong, just as your physical body requires food and water to maintain energy and endurance.

## Our Need to Be Centered in God

Yes, it's true that our heavenly Father knows what's in our hearts without a word from us (Matt. 6:8). But He wants us to bring our concerns, our burdens to Him (Matt. 7:7-8; Phil. 4:6; 1 Thess. 5:17-18). He wants an active relationship with us, and that means both talking to Him and listening—giving, not just receiving.

Surrounded by people who need and expect things from us, staggering under a load of responsibility, it's easy to feel overwhelmed. So we need that two-way communication to remind us who we are:

- Our lives are in His control, even when it seems everything in them is topsy-turvy.
- Our children are in His hand, even though they're growing up in a world where it seems human standards have sunk to the pits.
- He is the God who was there at the beginning, is with us now, and who will remain after everything else is gone.
- His Word strengthens us in our inner beings (Eph. 3:16-19).

In the midst of turmoil, you can remain serene and tranquil. Compare it to a raging storm on the ocean's surface, while the ocean depths remain calm and untroubled. In just the same way, when your depths are filled with the solid truth of God's Word, you'll have peace within yourself (Is. 26:3). Drawing on the Source of love, you'll be better equipped to handle crying babies and crayon pictures on the walls and spilled milk and frogs in pockets and teenage tantrums—with love.

Be assured that you'll not lose the time you give to the Lord! He will give it back—and then some, because you'll function so much more smoothly. Vicky has found this to be true.

"My children come home from school at 4 p.m., and my husband about an hour later," she says. "Those predinner hours used to drive me up the wall! But I've found a better way. I discovered that I really need to be in the presence of the Lord about 3 p.m. if I'm to be any good in the presence of my family for the rest of the evening. That quiet time somehow renews me so that I'm able to handle all the clamor and the demands in a loving way. When I miss it, my whole family notices the difference!"

## Talk Faith!

*V*icky's family knows the source of her strength. Does yours? If our faith is to be transferable, we need to weave it into the warp and woof of everyday life, everyday conversation. For example, when arriving at one's destination, instead of saying, "Well, we made it!" you could say, "The Lord got us here safely, didn't He?" When your three-year-old proudly brings you a dandelion, instead of saying, "Oh, what a pretty flower!" you could say, "God gives us so many beautiful growing things, doesn't He?" (Take a close look—you'll discover that even those pesky dandelions, if considered objectively, *are* beautiful!)You needn't preach a sermon. But when the occasion arises, quietly share with your children that you depend on the Lord; share your awareness of His blessings in daily life. And don't think that your witness is lost on your children—or your grandchildren.

One little girl surprised her Sunday school teacher by kneeling during the opening prayer. "Why, Shana, you don't have to kneel in order to talk to Jesus," said the teacher.

"Maybe not," said five-year-old Shana, who'd just come back from a weekend visit to her grandmother's home. "But this is the way my grandma talks to Jesus every morning, and I want to, too."

Let your children know that you bring them and their needs before God. Although they may never admit it, knowing that you're praying for them when they have a tough exam or that you're asking God to bring about a reconciliation with their best friend is comforting—and faith building, too, as they see how God meets their needs.

### The Hand That Rocks the Cradle . . .

*N*ever lose sight of this time-tested fact: You're not just raising children. You are growing people! Building and shepherding future adults who will found the families and shape the world of tomorrow. That's your delightful privilege—and your heavy responsibility. The smallest act, the most tiresome chore carries lasting significance.

Consequently, it's comforting to remember that you're not in this mothering business alone. The God who made you and your children walks with you every step of the way, so saturate your parenting with prayer. Pray for your baby before birth. Pray as you feed your infant. Pray over your daughter or son's bed as you give that last evening tuck-in to a sleeping child. Pray through your child's difficult phases and expect God to guide and enable. Pray for your child's friends. Pray your child into (and through) adolescence and teens.

Thank God for the child He has given you. Ask not that God will make your child what you consider perfect. Rather ask that God will enable your child to fulfill the potential the Maker built in.

Pray for yourself—that God will make you the mother He wants you to be. Pray for an honest, open spirit. Pray for wisdom, strength, humor—whatever you perceive as deficiencies in yourself or in your mothering. Pray that God will forge an unshakable bond between you and your child—one which becomes a friendship that warms and cheers you both.

It's not as some have said: When all else fails, pray. Rather, it's pray *first*. You can silently talk to your heavenly Father all through the day—in your normal routines as well as in your time of prayer. Let it become as natural as breathing. Expect Him to meet your needs, and then remember to thank Him when He does. "Every good and perfect gift is from above, coming down from the Father of the heavenly lights, who does not change like shifting shadows" (James 1:17).

Like all mothers you want a relationship with your children that grows and lasts for life. The place to start is with your own relationship with Christ. Make that your base, for (like it or not) what you are and think and feel will likely be reproduced—sooner or later—in your child.

Becoming a mother is the easy part. Being a mother 24 hours a day, 7 days a week, 52 weeks a year . . . that's the hard part! You need a solid base, an energy source, a power supply that never fails.

And you'll have it as you draw on the Lord's strength. Talk with Him, read His Word. Trust Him. Building on that sure foundation, the relationship you build with your child will be full and rich and lasting!

# 2

# *Of Birthing and Bonding*
## *The Vital Preschool Years*

Jesus said, "Let the little children
come to me, and do not hinder them,
for the kingdom of heaven belongs
to such as these."
      Matt. 19:14

We can't give our children the future,
strive though we may to make it secure.
But we can give them the present.
      Kathleen Norris

The love of a mother for her child is more
important than all of the scientific
information she may acquire about how to raise
that child. And the love of a mother for her
child is more important than all the common
sense she may have about how to raise that
child. . . . So mother, in the final analysis,
believe your own heart!
      Dr. Fitzhugh Dodson

People who say they sleep like a baby
usually don't have one.
      Leo J. Burke

Remember how having a baby is depicted in old movies and on television? Watch an "I Love Lucy" rerun if you've forgotten. Ricky paces the waiting room floor while hospital personnel whisk Lucy off to deliver little Ricky in a sterile—and lonely—delivery room. Later Ricky can only wave at his son through the glass of the strictly-off-limits nursery.

In those days—and probably when you were born—nobody worried about "bonding," but today it has become a catchword. The experts herald their latest findings via books and TV. Prospective mothers worry that something may interfere with this once-in-a-lifetime opportunity.

Mothers of children born before bonding made the news feel that they've somehow cheated their offspring and themselves of something very precious. Chances are that your own mother, like Lucy Ricardo, delivered you without the aid and comfort of your father—and she may have been heavily sedated, besides. She likely feels that she missed out on a lot more than pain. Were you scarred for life? she may wonder. Was your relationship measurably less than it could have been—if only she had known?

Well, how about it? What's all the fuss about bonding?

First of all, those who haven't "bonded" with their newborn have *not* forever missed their chance for a close relationship with their child. Relationships between people are seldom lost—and are never won for all time—in the space of an hour or two. The days and weeks and years that follow a child's birth are what counts. The best start can be blotted out by what comes after—and the worst start can develop into a warm, close parent-child relationship. So if you're one of those mothers, relax!

Current theory has it that the first hour or so following the birth of the child is the optimum time to establish the initial bond between parents and child. That includes delivery by Caesarean section. It's thought that such early time together in some way "imprints" the parents to the child and vice versa. (There's a similar process in the animal kingdom.) If mother and father are allowed time alone with their newborn (a minimum of 30 to 45 minutes, up to an hour or two), their bonding as a family is enhanced for life, say researchers such as Drs. Marshall Klaus and John Kennell. New parents are encouraged to have lots of eye-to-eye contact, to stroke and fondle their infant, and to count fingers and toes. Mother holds her baby against her bare abdomen and puts the child to her breast. Such skin-to-skin contact is considered especially beneficial at this time. Klaus and Kennell believe that this introduction can have an important effect on fashioning the parent-child relationship.

## *Touch and Talk Aid Development*

Once you're back home and in the months that follow, keep your baby near you during waking hours. The sight and sound of you is both reassuring and stimulating to the infant. Talk to little Jessica as you change her diaper, even though she doesn't yet respond. Smile and talk to Zachary as you feed him and care for him, even *before* he smiles back. This interaction, even though it appears one-sided, enhances the child's ability to learn to relate to people.

As you interact with your child in everyday life, your small daughter or son will learn to trust and depend on you. That's true whether you're a full-time homemaker or employed outside the home. Even when your time together is limited, the same time-tested principles apply.

Babies and young children need lots of care; that's a given. Try not to view these duties as "chores," but rather as built-in opportunities. Every diaper change, every feeding—every day—is another building block in the foundation of your relationship with your child. The strong bond you establish during your child's first year of life will help ensure that the two of you can together ride out the crises and trying situations which may arise later on.

So make the most of these early months—of the seemingly endless feeding and tending and holding. Give your child your full attention. Be there emotionally, as well as bodily. When you pick up a fussy baby, for example, carry on a conversation, even though you do all the talking:

"I'll bet you're hungry, aren't you?"

"Do you need your diaper changed?"

"Are you tired of your crib?"

The words aren't important, but the interaction is.

Most adults instinctively encourage little ones to respond. In the presence of a baby or toddler we're likely to foolishly prattle on:

"Can you give Mommy a big smile?"

"Where's your nose?"

"Can you say Ma-ma?"

And that's good—keep it up! When your child reciprocates with a smile, a giggle, or with sound, be liberal with your encouragement. Your praise reinforces the child's desire to repeat the performance. Mothers who give ample oral stimulation not only enhance the mother-child bond but also foster their child's emotional development and communication skills.

Speak your love frequently. It's *easy* to tell a baby or a young child, "I love you." Even if the words aren't understood, the look on your face will say it all. Verbalize your love all through your child's growing up years, and it will still be natural and comfortable when your offspring is a touchy teen.

Don't worry about "spoiling" your child in this first year. Hold your infant frequently. Babies who are hugged often, who are kissed and caressed and patted, thrive. (They cry less, too.) That's why parents of premature infants are encouraged to visit the hospital, to touch and stroke their baby, even though the preemie may not be allowed out of the incubator. Children, like adults, need human touch and interaction to flourish.

This would seem to be an argument in favor of carrying your infant in one of those cuddler-type carriers, rather than toting Baby around in some sort of rigid infant seat. Holding your infant may be awkward and even tiring, but it seems less so when you remember that you're actually nourishing your child emotionally.

By the way, it's not too early to introduce your child to Jesus. For instance, if you have a picture of Christ on the wall, hold the baby up to it and say:

"See Jesus, Zachary? Jesus *loves* Zachary!"

"Who is this, Jessica? Jesus? That's right, Jesus *loves* Jessica!"

"This is your Best Friend, Zachary. What's His name? Yes, it's Jesus!"

Give your young child the priceless gift of knowing from the beginning that Jesus Christ loves him or her. That knowledge provides an added measure of security, even at a very young age.

## *Your Child Is One of a Kind*

**M**uch has been written about the importance of a child's first five years—the most significant in emotional and intellectual development. But even in the first year the very young child forms an opinion that the world is either good or bad and adopts an attitude which is (or isn't) optimistic and expectant. During this period the child learns whether Mother gives love without conditions: I love you, and I'll take care of you, just because you're my child—or whether there are strings attached.

Realize that your baby is an individual from the moment of birth—and respect that uniqueness. Some babies love to cuddle; some pull away. Sleeping patterns, too, are highly individual. Some infants seem to have been "born happy," others are fretful from their first day of life. Some babies are calm and placid, others wriggle constantly, startle easily, and never seem to settle down. If you're a parent who thought you were getting a nice, pliable lump of human clay to mold into your dream child, you're in for a shock.

"Early on I knew Sarah would be a handful," says Sharon. "It was January, and I had to bundle her up for the drive home from the hospital. Well, I put on her cap, and she turned red and started yelling. That was the beginning . . .

"I breastfed her and soon ran out of people who would babysit because she would *never* take a bottle—just hollered till I got home. When I weaned her, she screamed for 24 hours before she gave in to a bottle feeding. By then we were both a wreck. Sarah's really not a spoiled child. She's simply had a mind of her own since she opened her eyes!"

Jill smiles in understanding. "Our first boy, Timmy, was such an easy baby. He smiled all the time and slept a lot, and we just loved him to pieces. We thought, 'Hey, if raising kids is this easy, let's have a dozen!' Then we had Joey . . ." she sighs. "Joey has fussed and fidgeted from his first moment of life. I think he came out yelling! He didn't sleep all night till he was a year old, and he gave up his morning nap by the time he was six months old. He's two now and never sits still a minute—takes apart everything he gets his hands on.

"I truly love him—but I'm continually bushed. How could the same parents have two kids as different as night and day? Joey is definitely our last child. And if he'd been our first, he probably would have been our *only* child!"

Ask any parent of more than one youngster, and they'll likely tell you a similar tale. Each child is unique, unpredictable, full of strengths and weaknesses. Human. The only one who really knows your child and can predict what this bundle of humanity can become is the Creator. Parents can help their children to develop their potential, can learn to maximize strengths and minimize weaknesses, can offer unqualified love and support. Perhaps you can smooth off some of the rough edges. But you cannot make your child into your own (or anyone else's) image.

Isn't that exciting? Think how dull it would be if they were predictable—or if one child was just like another!

So give your child the precious freedom to develop as an individual.

Don't lay on your child the burden of your own dreams, either. Lee Anne yearned to become a ballerina all through childhood, but her parents refused to drive her into the city for lessons. So she determined to do the next best thing: get the finest instruction for her own daughter, Tracey. She bought Tracey's first pair of ballet slippers when the baby was just a few months old and hung pictures of dancers in the nursery. Lee Anne bought picture books and stories of ballerinas and went through them with the toddling Tracey.

"All my life I knew I must dance," says Tracey. "Mom often told me how much she had wanted to be a ballerina and that now I must dance in her place. She'd describe to me how beautiful and graceful I would look as I danced *Swan Lake*. She simply never understood that I wasn't coordinated, that I hated the whole idea. *I dreamed of being another Madame Curie!*

"I finally dropped out, and Mom pretended that it didn't matter . . . but there was always a sadness in her eyes. Her dream was gone for good, I guess. I earned my M.S. degree, and now I really am a researcher—and I love it! Yet somehow I feel that I've never quite measured up."

When children know that their parents think they're okay as they are, they're much more apt to like themselves. If you appreciate your daughter or son as is, unconditionally, you'll establish a climate in your home wherein each child can blossom to the fullest. The youngster will develop a healthy self-image and will feel loved and secure with you, the parent(s).

Come to think of it, isn't that exactly what our heavenly Father does for us?

## Mutual Respect Begins Early

Such acceptance is a key component of respect. We all want our children to respect us. Some parents demand it, but that's seldom the way to get it. Rather, children learn to give respect when they receive it themselves. For instance: You teach them to say please and thank you; return the courtesy. You want them to knock before entering your room; do the same before you enter their bedrooms. You expect them to be considerate of other people; be thoughtful of their feelings and self-image, too. Never ridicule your children or label them, either privately or in front of others. For example, parents may make remarks such as these to friends:

"Susie is such a crybaby."

"Tommy just can't learn the way his big brother can."

"Aaron is afraid of strangers."

"Jessica is our beauty, and Heidi has the brains."

What difference do such casual remarks make? As Grandma used to say, "Little pitchers have big ears." Children hear and remember, then adopt these descriptions as mental identification tags: Stupid Tommy Smith. And Tommy Smith may wear that millstone for life.

Another part of respect is to accept your child's feelings. For instance, when Zachary doesn't want to sit on Uncle Ralph's lap or Jessica is terrified of the neighbor's dog, don't simply say, "Oh, of course, you don't mean that!" To children, such feelings are real—and very important. You can show that you understand by putting those feelings into your own words and feeding them back to the child. Take the time to talk it through with the child, but acknowledge his or her right to have emotions that may seem illogical to you. Be supportive and loving, then see how your children gain in confidence, how their trust in you will grow.

## Learning Is Day-to-Day

*I*t all goes back again to the maxim: More is caught than taught.
Children learn to love by being loved.

Children learn to trust when parents prove trustworthy. *Always* be honest, even if you could temporarily avoid a fuss by shading the truth.

Children develop their self-image mostly by perceiving how others, especially parents, perceive them.

An excellent discussion of the feedback method known as P.E.T. is Earl Gaulke's *You Can Have a Family Where Everybody Wins: Christian Perspectives on Parent Effectiveness Training* (St. Louis: Concordia Publishing House, 1975).

And you are teaching every minute of every day . . . by your facial expression and tone of voice, as well as by your words.

"Oh, great!" says Laura. "Just what I need—a guilt trip! Listen, I can barely keep up now. My nine-month-old son still gets me up during the night, my two-and-one-half-year-old boy will probably never get out of diapers, and my five-year-old wets the bed once or twice a week. I work at least 16 hours a day, nonstop. I fall into bed at night, and I drag myself out of bed in the morning. Now I'm supposed to watch the expression on my face and my tone of voice, too? Come on! Gimme a break and get off my case!"

Laura's feelings—and lifestyle—are typical of overburdened mothers of young children. Unless you're blessed to have accommodating relatives nearby, most find the physical and emotional demands of mothering a constant, exhausting drain. So where is one supposed to discover the energy to put all these lovely theories into practice?

## A Tale of Two Families

*T*he secret is in your attitude, and that's something you alone control. Let's consider two hypothetical families as an illustration:

In Family A when three-year-old Jessica spills something, Mom might say, "Must you *always* spill your milk on my clean floor? You are so clumsy! You're always spilling things and knocking things over!"

In Family B Mother doesn't react much to spills, except to help quietly clean up the mess and to give the embarrassed spiller a reassuring smile and a pat.

When four-year-old Zachary misbehaves, the mother in Family A may say something like, "You are a *bad* boy. You're always getting into trouble. No, you can't sit on my lap! I don't want to hold a bad boy. You just go play by yourself until you can be nice!"

In Family B, Mother deals quickly with the misbehavior by administering a discipline method of her choice. Then she hugs Aaron or holds him on her lap and says, "I didn't like what you did, but I really love you, Aaron, and I know that you want to do what's right. You just have some learning to do. I forgive you because I know that Jesus forgives *me* when I do bad things. So let's forget about this now and be happy." (This is also an excellent time to offer a simple prayer asking Jesus to help both child and mother to be what He wants them to be.)

It's easy to see, isn't it, that the mother in Family B doesn't take any more time—or energy—and probably less. Certainly it costs her less in terms of emotion. She also preserves or builds the child's self-image. You see, a major factor in strengthening the mother-child relationship—from the beginning of your child's life—is this mutual respect and consideration and your unconditional acceptance. As with so many other things, you get back what you give out.

In short, *you* set the style. Your own attitude determines whether your family is more like A or more like B. To be sure, you're allowed some annoyance when a child misbehaves. You're human, after all. But if you're wise, you'll expect that youngsters inevitably act up and spill things, so you won't overreact when such everyday mishaps occur. When one of your primary aims is to build a balanced self-concept in your child, you'll avoid name-calling or labeling; you'll punish misdeeds; but you'll never withdraw—or threaten to withdraw—your love from your child. And it's necessary for you to think this through early on, to get it settled in your mind once and for all. Because no matter what your words, the look on your face, the tone of your voice will—as they always do—communicate what you're feeling inside.

Be aware, too, that children don't differentiate between themselves and their behavior. For example, when Mom tells Jessica that she's clumsy, she means that Jessica is okay, but she does spill her milk and run into chairs. But Jessica interprets it (and believes it, deep down,) that her *whole being* is clumsy, i.e.: "I do clumsy things because I'm a clumsy *person*." Children adopt your careless label as a description and identification. And it takes many, many positive statements to overcome just one negative remark.

## *Do Away with Destructive Patterns*

Analyze the parenting you received as a child. Perhaps your own family resembled Family A. If so, when your offspring act childishly, your built-in reaction will be to repeat the same old cycle. You need a new role model. Is there a Christian mother, either your age or older, whom you admire? Do you wish that your children's behavior and your own style of mothering were more like hers?

Why not go to her and tell her that you sincerely yearn to emulate her as a mother? Ask her if she would be your mentor.

"Fran kind of took me under her wing," says Debbie, "and I've really learned a lot from her. Sometimes she'll scold, 'No, no, no, that's not the way to do it!' But she says it with a big grin, so I don't mind. And if I disagree or have a question, I just say so. She's been a lifesaver to me a hundred times. My mom lives halfway across the country, and besides, I don't want to be the kind of mother she was. So when I'm stumped, I call Fran. Her boys are in the upper grades, while my girls are still preschoolers. I can see that Fran's ways work because I know how her family operates. I really thank the Lord for putting us in the same place at the same time."

Along with finding an understanding friend, you'll want to break free from negative responses that were programmed into you as a child. But where does one go to get old memories purged, to obtain a temperament transplant? How does one become inwardly sure and solid? For that matter where does one turn when the everyday demands of life seem overwhelming?

For lasting inward change we need to bring our fears and failures, our sins and our insecurities, our mental hangups and our painful memories before our merciful Father. Dredge them up from within, even though it hurts. Name them before God and ask Him to take them from you for the sake of Jesus Christ, who died to set you free. Ask God's Holy Spirit to give you a new heart, a new mind-set. "Therefore, if anyone is in Christ, he is a new creation; the old has gone, the new has come!" (2 Cor. 5:17).

Then depend on Him to make you what you need to be as you rear the children He has entrusted to you. "If any of you lacks wisdom, he should ask God, who gives generously to all without finding fault, and it will be given to him"(James 1:5). "And my God will meet all your needs according to His glorious riches in Christ Jesus"(Phil. 4:19).

## *The Sticky Question*

*T*he jury is still out—and probably will be for many years—on the ultimate effect of a growing lifestyle: mothers who are employed outside the home. If you're at home full-time, consider yourself blessed. (Many employed mothers wish they could be, too.) But don't kid yourself that your mere presence in the home somehow guarantees well-balanced offspring.

For example: Jill resents being tied down with a baby, a four-year-old, and a second-grader. She loves her children and aims to be what they need her to be, but she's often frustrated and feels "stuck." Her children receive good care, but they're whiny and fretful. Whenever Mommy leaves the house, they cry long and loud, which only increases Jill's feeling that she's a prisoner in her own home. The key, of course, is that her children sense her "hidden" irritation and feel insecure about her love for them.

Mothers employed outside the home, on the other hand, often work hard to promote a sense of stability in their children. They may strive to verbalize their love more often, to show their support in every way they can so that their youngsters won't feel short-changed.

Precisely because their hours with their children are limited, they prize that time. Whether such "quality time" makes up for limited quantity is not yet either proven or unproven. Each mother must reach her own prayerful decision.

The point is that being home is not invariably better, nor is working outside the home always a detriment. Many mothers find that part-time employment proves to be an excellent compromise. "I love it!" says Shelley. "I get out enough to keep me sane, and I'm home enough not to lose touch with my kids. For me it's the perfect answer."

If you're an employed mother, you'll have to locate a mother substitute. It's obvious, but not always considered, that you need to find a person with whom you feel compatible. This woman will probably spend more waking hours with your child than you and will play a major part in helping to form the child's personality. So you'll want to have similar views on discipline, attitudes, and faith, as well as on what to feed young children. When you've narrowed down your choices, don't be too casual. Ask questions—lots of them. If you could find a committed Christian, you'd immediately agree on many things. If that's not possible, be sure you know the ways in which you agree and differ. Can you live with that? Are you comfortable with the arrangement? Do you have a rapport between the two of you?

Once children are in school, many mothers go back to full-time employment. It's understandably tempting to want to save money on babysitting and allow your children to join the multitude of "latchkey kids." After all, *your* children are reliable. But spending that time alone, day after day, is lonely—and risky, besides.

Persist until you locate trustworthy after-school care and consider the cost a good investment. Take your time choosing, until you're entirely satisfied. It will pay off in your peace of mind and in your children's emotional stability. Is there an at-home mother who might welcome this opportunity to supervise your children and pick up some extra income? Consider advertising your need at church. Some Christian women see this as a special ministry—which it is.

The idealistic dreams of pregnancy dissipate rapidly when exposed to a real baby who cries, who may be colicky, and who seems determined to be a night owl forever. A baby turns out to be a 24-hour-a-day proposition.

So is developing and strengthening the bond between you and your child. But it has value that will endure—for both of you—for life!

## *Pulling It All Together*

*M*othering is hard work, especially if your child is an infant or a young child. Days are long, sleep is often short and interrupted. You can't find a corner of your home, not even your bathroom, where some little person won't be standing outside (or traipsing through) and calling, "Mommy!" Whatever else you do, you're always a mother—24 hours a day, seven days a week. That being on call everyday alone constitutes a pressure that can be overwhelming at times.

Yet you also experience joy as your child grows. You feel satisfaction and delight as you note each milestone in development. These emotions are just as real. They just get overlooked as you tend to the day-to-day demands of living. Sadly, we sometimes fail even to notice.

Obviously you are reading this book because your heart's aim is to build a strong, lasting relationship with your child. And this is the very best time to begin that process. So here's a quick summary of this chapter. There are of course many more facets to optimum mothering. But these basics can help to build a secure foundation for the strong mother-child relationship you want. And they're good habits to form because the same principles apply to parenting children of all ages.

- *Choose* to adopt a cheerful, calm attitude. Don't view yourself as buried under responsibilities but rather as a developer of balanced, healthy persons.
- Nourish your child emotionally. Hold your baby often. Caress, kiss, and hug your infant and young child frequently.
- Keep your infant near you.
- "Be there" when you feed and care for your child, even the newborn. Give him or her your full attention—talk and smile and enjoy.

- Give your love without conditions—I love you because you *are* (not because you're obedient or smart or talented or beautiful).
- Don't forget to say, "I love you." Children like to hear those three words as much as adults.
- Recognize and accept your offspring's God-given uniqueness. Don't try to remake your child into your concept of "the perfect child."
- In every way you can, nurture and build your child's self-image.
- Give respect if you want to receive it.
- Expect your child to behave as a child.
- Remember: More is caught than taught.
- Find a mother whose style or children you admire. Ask her to be your friend and mentor. (She will be complimented. How could she refuse?)
- Depend on your faithful God to meet your needs as you continually take them to Him in prayer.

**For Further Reading:**

Brazelton, T. Berry, M.D. *On Becoming a Family.* Delacorte Press, 1981. Many photos and personal studies of birthing and bonding and early months of life.

Dobson, Dr. James. *Dare to Discipline.* Tyndale, 1970. Christian-oriented; over one million copies have been sold. Dobson is well known for his radio and TV programs.

──────────── . *Hide or Seek.* Revell, 1974. Christian-oriented; tells how to build self-esteem in children from birth into teens.

──────────── . *The Strong-Willed Child.* Tyndale, 1978. Christian-oriented; discusses parenting the assertive or defiant child from birth through adolescence.

Dodson, Dr. Fitzhugh. *How to Parent.* New American Library, 1970. A standard; sensible, detailed information on ages and stages, plus suitable play equipment, etc., ages 1-5.

Johnson, Spencer, M.D. *The One-Minute Mother.* Morrow, 1983. Basic principles of child-training, simply stated, that will improve mother-child communication and build child's self-esteem; easy-to-follow procedures for goals, praise, and reprimands.

Meier, Paul D. and Linda Burnett. *The Unwanted Generation*. Baker Book, 1980. Christian-oriented; thorough discussion of day care, strongly weighted against (with much corroborating material), but also some advice for choosing care-givers.

Rakowitz, Elly and Gloria S. Rubin. *Living with Your New Baby*. Watts, 1978. Preparation for birth, birth process, and accompanying physiological changes, emotions of parents, etc.; practical.

# 3
# Mother or Chauffeur?
## Keeping Up with the Grade-Schooler

*The God to whom small boys pray has a face very much like their mother's.*
  *James Barrie*

*If a child lives with approval, he learns to live with himself.*
  *Dorothy Law Nolte*

*You can never go wrong by giving a youngster lots of love and kisses mixed with discipline. Child training is merely knowing which end of your child to pat . . . and when.*
  *Jan Marshall*

*The woman who creates and sustains a home, and under whose hands children grow up to be strong and pure men and women, is a creator second only to God.*
  *Helen Hunt Jackson*

*Before I got married I had six theories about bringing up children; now I have six children and no theories.*
  *Earl of Rochester 1647-1680*

Life, they say, consists of phases. If mothering a baby is exhausting (and it is)—if chasing after a toddler leaves you breathless (and it does)—if answering the endless questions of a preschooler puts you in a dither (and it will)—then all will be wonderful when your child is in school. Won't it?

Well, not exactly. For one thing, you discover that you're no longer the unchallenged expert. Nor do you remain the center of your child's world. Whereas Matthew used to brag, "My mom says . . ," now every other sentence begins, "Well, Mrs. Smith says . . ."

It doesn't bother *you*, of course. After all, you're a reasonable adult. Nevertheless, you feel a twinge of loss? envy? annoyance? as the days and weeks go on. You're still mother and child, but you sense that something precious—a quality you had undervalued—now will be forever missing from your relationship.

Not so long ago you had cabin fever from being cooped up too long with pint-sized folk who seldom uttered complete sentences. Now you find yourself hauling carloads of youngsters across town and back again, often several times a day. You long for more time at home with the children (just your own, please!), together and uninterrupted.

Welcome to the "one of these days I'll look down and find that I've sprouted wheels where my legs used to be" stage. Enter Mom the chauffeur.

And so we bustle about, feeling frazzled but smug as we give our children "all the advantages." Sad to say, we may be giving them the good, while they miss out on the best. Skills and straight teeth are terrific, but they don't provide a solid base on which to build a life. Nor do they ensure emotional equilibrium. That comes from the simple basics on which individual and family strength have always been established: unconditional love, acceptance, honesty, affirmation, a shared, living faith in God. Those are the same factors, by the way, that nourish your own lifetime relationship with your child.

Since your child was born, you've been laying the groundwork. If you've been building carefully, with Jesus Christ as your foundation, you're on the right track (1 Cor. 3:10-11). As children grow up, you employ the same sound principles you put into practice earlier. The form may need to be modified or expanded, but the same fundamental truths apply.

## *The Many Ways of Love*

Someone has said that each of us wears an invisible sign that reads, "Please Love Me." That's why the bedrock of a strong family—and of the child's self-image and security, probably for life—is unconditional, accepting, affirming love. Jesus admonished His followers to love each other, and that carries over into our families. *The Living Bible* paraphrases John 15:17-18a like this: [Jesus says:] "I demand that you love each other, for you get enough hate from the world!"

All of us, parents and children alike, get enough hate and hostility, enough carping and criticism, from the circles in which we move. Children's peers, in fact, can be downright cruel. The everyday world is rightly likened to a battleground more often than to an oasis of peace. So it's imperative that within our own families we give and receive unqualified love and unlimited affirmation. If not there, where? Who will nurture us if not those closest to us?

Every human being hungers to know that the love-giver attaches no strings. Children are especially vulnerable. So, as an example, we don't say (or imply), "*If* you're a good girl, Mommy will love you," or, "How can you expect me to love you *when* you disappoint me so often? How can I be proud of you *when* you're naughty?"

Anything in that vein is really saying, "I will love you *if* . . . ." As Christians, we of all people should see the inconsistency of accepting Christ's love for us while we were yet sinners, while expecting our children to be "good" first before we will love them.

So tell your children, often, that you love them. Then demonstrate it by your actions. Some parents fear that if they're not stern and cold when children misbehave, the youngsters will infer that their parents actually approve of their wrong behavior. Not true! The child knows the difference. So aim to model yourself after Jesus Christ, loving and forgiving your child. And when you forgive, be sure to forget, also. Don't trot out your list of old grievances when other problems arise.

Be aware that sometimes children "act up" because they're feeling insecure. This happens when you bring the new baby home from the hospital and Matthew suddenly turns into a brat. (Presumably you'll have prepared Matthew well in advance, read him books about how babies are born, let him feel the baby kicking, let him help you pick out layette items, and so forth. Even so, most children exhibit temporary insecurity and need lots of extra TLC—during a period when you're hard-pressed just to provide care. All Matthew knows for sure is the evidence of his own eyes: you spend all your time caring and feeding and cuddling that intruder who cries all the time. Who can blame him for feeling threatened?)

Carleen, mother of five boys, found a way to lessen this sibling rivalry. "When our second son was born, I needed to keep his toddler brother within view while I cared for the baby. So I started telling Danny how lucky he was to have such a super big brother. I told the baby that Patrick was *so* smart, *so* clever, *such* a loving little boy, *such* a good helper to Mommy. Why, Patrick could walk and feed himself and bring in the mail and put away his toys . . . on and on I went.

"Well, it was magic!" continues Carleen, laughing. "Every time I fed Danny, Patrick would come running to hear how great *he* was and how much Fred and I loved him! The baby was delighted, too, because I talked *to* the baby—but *about* his big brother.

"With each new baby I did the same. I told the newest kid about all the other kids. The whole crew would drop what they were doing and gather around. They'd just sit there, grinning. It was such a special time for all of us! No resentment problems at all because of a new baby. In fact, the others were always sorry when the baby began feeding himself!

"Actually, I think listening to all the positive stuff I said about them gave them something to live up to. Their minds were open, and I could regularly drop in images of obedience and helpfulness and harmony and love . . . It was good for me, too. Reminded me I had great kids!"

Acting up can also occur when Kara achieves some honor or praise, and then Cassie wonders whether that means you love Kara more than her. Though it seems like perverse reasoning, children sometimes show their hunger for reassurance of your love by testing you. They long to hear you *say* that you love them no matter what. (Just as we grownups need to hear those three words from our spouses!)

Parents sometimes fall into the habit of giving their children attention only when they're misbehaving or being disruptive. Yet if good behavior is consistently overlooked or children feel ignored, they may disobey just to get *some* kind of attention, even if it's negative. They'd rather be punished than ignored. So aim to "catch your children in the act" of behaving appropriately. Then praise them; affirm them. And let it be for something ordinary, not always for achievements that are infrequent (such as getting an "A" in Math) or outstanding (such as hitting a home run).

It's worth repeating: accept each child as a unique person. If you observe sibling rivalry, realize that it's a standard condition, even in the happiest of families. Just don't intensify the competition by comparing one child to another. For example, Matthew may be an honor roll student who seems seldom to hit the books. Yet brother Kyle may remain a C student, even when he really works hard.

If you hold Matthew up as an example for Kyle, one of two things will happen. Either Kyle will be trying—and—failing—all through his growing-up years and will feel second class. ("Matt's grades are so good; there's no use in my trying to catch up. I guess I'm just dumb!") Or he'll set out to be totally unlike his brother and will automatically reject whatever Matthew is and does. ("Matt's such a goody-goody. Well, not me!") Animosity between Kyle and Matthew is guaranteed.

## *Have You Hugged Your Kid Today?*

*A*nd that means boys as well as girls. In fact, some counselors feel that boys are more often behavior problems partly because we hold back displays of affection, afraid that we'll turn them into sissies. Some parents even fear that too much touching could impart a distorted attitude toward sexuality. Not to worry. We're talking about showing appropriate love here, which will not do that. But it *will* build the inner strength and security you want your child to have and free this young person to be all that God intends.

Perhaps all this talk of touching to show affection makes you a mite uncomfortable, because you didn't come out of "that kind" of background. Maybe you don't like anyone to get too close—not even your spouse, except for sexual contact. If so, ask the Lord to help you to be more open and less self-conscious. Because it isn't just children who hunger for love and touching. We adults have the same needs; we just know how to hide them better!

Your tone of voice and the words you use, too, have a lot to do with whether your home "feels" loving. Listen to yourself and your spouse, to your interaction with your children, with the same attention you'd pay when visiting in someone else's home.

"My cousin and her husband would walk through fire for their kids," says Billie, "but you'd never know it from watching and listening to them in action! The four of them yell at each other all the time. I'm sure they don't even hear themselves anymore. Just the same, if I were one of those kids, I don't think I'd feel very loved!"

Some parents would respond, "Well, that's just my way. It doesn't mean anything!"

True, it's an intangible. But how we speak and how we act *does* make a difference. Why not treat your children with the same courtesy you'd show to an outsider? Ridiculous? Not at all. With a guest you'd be careful not to hurt that person's feelings. You'd listen when you were bored, laugh when you were not amused, be pleasant when you felt impatient. We expect family members, however, to take us as we are, which may be felt as inconsiderate and uncaring.

Never assume that because children are older, their egos are less fragile. In fact, the reverse is probably true. Your aim is to be supportive and to affirm your child. The pictures that children form of themselves, their self-respect (or lack of it), are drawn largely from how they *think* their parents view them.

## *Make Time, Mother*

*T*ime has a way of evaporating. Don't let it! Plan time with each child individually, *every* day if possible. You can play games or read aloud or just talk. But whether it's 5 minutes or 30, give your un-

47

divided attention during that time period. You want your child to feel, "Right now I must be the most important person there is to my mom." And that private time goes a long way toward establishing close communication. You'll find that you not only "hear the news" but also get a glimpse into what your child is feeling and thinking as your child's confidence grows and communication becomes more comfortable.

How do you handle it when you observe that your child is upset? Sometimes youngsters openly tell you that they have a problem or are worried or afraid. But more likely they'll send out nonverbal messages, and it will be up to you to pick up the clues. You may find that they're extra quiet or irritable or antisocial. The manifestations may vary, but the root cause is usually the same: they hurt.

You can often encourage sharing by gently saying, "I've been wondering if something's bothering you lately." Choose a time when the home atmosphere is calm and you have some time. Add a smile and a reassuring touch. But you need to proceed with caution here and do some self-examination beforehand.

What's your customary reaction when your children do share their anxieties with you? Suppose, for example, that Matthew is afraid he won't make the Little League team. Do you immediately jump in with the solution? "Guess you'll just have to spend more time practicing." Do you minimize what this means to Matthew? "Oh, well, lots of kids don't play ball, and they have a good time anyhow." Do you criticize? "Look, if you wouldn't fool around so much, you'd probably be good enough!" Do you sympathize? "Oh, honey, I'm *so* sorry! You must feel just terrible! You poor thing! Just for that, I'll go get a pizza with all the trimmings for dinner." Do you devalue? "You think *that's* bad! *I* have to worry about paying the bills! Just wait till you're grown up, and you'll find out what a real problem is!"

Obviously, the person of any age who gets answers like that will likely conclude, "That's the last time I *ever* tell her how I feel!"

Professional counselors tell us there's a better way. Learn to listen—with feeling. For instance, when Kara tells you that her best friend didn't invite her to the slumber party, don't try to cheer her up. Instead, allow her the feelings. You might respond, "You must really feel left out of the fun." That, of course, simply echoes what Kara said to you, but it also communicates that you heard the feelings behind the words.

In his book *You Can Have a Family Where Everybody Wins*, Earl Gaulke details one process of helpful listening: P.E.T. (Parent Effectiveness Training) from a Christian perspective. Gaulke notes that Christ "didn't simply dish out comforting words and good advice, but *entered into* our condition fully and completely" (p. 14). That's our task, too, as parents—to listen attentively, to feel *with* our children in their hurts and concerns (Rom. 12:15).

Unfortunately, we often suppose that parents are to function like Dear Abby, always ready with instant, pat answers to our children's problems. Yet our children, like you and me, will probably reject someone else's solution. Our reflective listening shows that we care; our support builds their confidence. Then they're much more able to arrive at an answer for themselves. Contradictory as it seems, this parental approach often leads children to ask our opinion more frequently, because they won't feel pressured. And, of course, if they *ask* our advice, they'll be more apt to listen and to ponder our reply.

Say it again: children develop the habit of talking to their parents when parents listen with an open mind, give their full attention, and don't interrupt. As the old saying goes: God gave us *two* ears and *one* mouth for a reason. Parents who learn to listen to their youngsters (and to hear them!) establish a climate of mutual respect in which their children—and their intercommunication—can flourish.

You may be looking forward a few years to your child's adolescence, wondering whether there'll be openness and sharing or secrecy and guardedness. Right now you hold the key to those years in your hand. If you don't have time to listen to your child today, don't expect that your teenager will have time to talk tomorrow.

Mealtimes can be a built-in opportunity for communication. Regrettably, in many families most of the interaction is a battle of wills: either Kara will lose (and gag on that last bite of spinach) or Kara will win (after a long harangue that makes everyone tense). In many homes the evening meal is the regular occasion for listing crime and punishment.

Why not make the dinner hour fun? Each family member could share the most pleasant thing that happened that day. Each could come prepared with a new joke or riddle or something learned that day. Mom and Dad or the older children might clip news items to discuss, or they could share an interesting fact. Some families play word games. Make your time together enjoyable, and you'll find that your children aren't so likely to gulp and go. They'll rather linger for the fun. And the good feelings engendered will reinforce satisfaction within the family.

Before dinner, however, comes that frenzied after-school, after-work period. Too often, hungry kids and uptight parents clash as whoever's cooking races with the clock. Yes, Virginia, there is a way out. Schedule an "attitude adjustment hour" and serve healthful snacks—celery and carrot sticks, cheese and crackers, juice, etc. Gather the family together in front of the fireplace or out on the patio and take time to unwind and to catch up on each other's news. You'll find this takes the edge off appetites (and tempers) and can be a very special family custom. Serve a simple supper later and save the big productions for the weekend.

## *Discipline as a Building Block*

*E*ven discipline can strenthen our mother-child relationship, but that presupposes that we have the proper understanding of the term. In its basic meaning, discipline is simply training a child in the way to live. The better disciplined your child, the less often you'll need to administer punishment. Surprised? Perhaps that's because most of us, sadly, consider discipline synonymous with some kind of penalty. Far from the truth! Your goal as a parent is to help your child achieve *self*-discipline in a measure that increases with each year. First comes inner security and then the control that comes from within oneself.

How do you grow a strong, self-reliant child? Do you maintain unswerving rules and keep a paddle handy? There are convincing arguments from "the experts," both pro and con. Dr. James Dobson considers spanking beneficial, and it is quick and decisive. Dr. Ross Campbell, on the other hand, believes that spanking, frequently employed, actually hinders the development of the child's conscience. Campbell maintains that the child regards the spanking as full payment for the crime, and thus feels no guilt. And although no one wants children consumed by remorse, he believes that a "healthy amount" of guilt is necessary to formulate and sustain the conscience. So to spank or not to spank remains a personal decision.

Another often-recommended method to evoke good conduct is behavior modification. You give a reward, such as a piece of candy, for good behavior and just ignore the bad. Sounds like a simple system, doesn't it? Applauding and reinforcing appropriate conduct is desirable, true. Nevertheless, "behavior mod" has some drawbacks. For example, what if Matthew isn't in the mood for jelly beans and so feels no desire to carry out your request?

A family is not a dictatorship, but it's not truly a democracy, either. The buck stops with you. So as a responsible Christian mother, you'll set clear limits, but you'll be fair. You'll be honest and consistent and take time to explain your reasoning. If forced to make changes, you'll keep your child informed. When necessary, you'll administer punishment. In all of it your primary goal is the development and ultimate welfare of your child. One-upmanship has no place in this relationship. And be liberal with love—before, during, and after.

With every method, what it finally comes down to is this: will the child, without any chance of immediate reward, without an authority figure keeping close watch, choose the right action? As Christian parents, that's what we all pray for. So you endeavor to discipline your children in a positive manner, to preserve and build their self-image, to model your love on the unconditional love of our Savior. Youngsters who feel truly secure in their parents' love want to measure up to expectations. Second, that strong bond of affection ensures that they'll respond to your guidance far more readily, without resentment.

Sometimes children baffle us with their behavior. The usually compliant child turns rebel. Another seems to be unusually peevish and quarrelsome. The key is to discover the feelings behind the actions and discern what your child needs. Think about recent family history. Has Matthew been a behavior problem lately because he's feeling forgotten or troubled? Is he having difficulty at school? If so, he doesn't need a scolding, but rather reassurance that he's deeply loved. Has Kara turned complainer because she's wondering whether you love her cute little sister more than her?

Think of misbehavior as a symptom, not the disease. When you deal with the root cause, the behavior problems will probably cease all by themselves. That doesn't mean that you overlook misconduct. It simply means that you first make sure your child feels firmly planted in your love and that you take time to evaluate each situation individually.

As for punishment, if you observe that your child is truly sorry, you may simply forgive, feeling that the child has learned the lesson. That's exactly what our Lord does for us when we have sorrow over sin, so it's certainly acceptable for us, too. Still, it's good for youngsters to discover that there are consequences to every action. When Matthew imitates Evel Knievel and damages the wheel on his bike, calmly explain that it's up to him to earn the money to fix it. Being without a bicycle for awhile will be sufficient punishment—and provide plenty of time to think.

In fact, it's a good principle of parenting: Let your children learn from natural consequences. When Matthew dawdles over breakfast, let him miss the schoolbus. When Kara doesn't do her homework, let her get an F. Cruel? Not at all, because all of us feel better about ourselves when we set our own goals and carry them out. Even first-graders can wake up to their own alarm clocks and be responsible for dressing, eating breakfast, and being ready on time. As for homework, if *you* take on the burden of seeing that it's done, you become the nag, and Kara won't begin until you remind her and keep checking up on her.

Yes, you expect only that which is within their capabilities, and you protect them from situations that could be harmful, either physically or emotionally. Do monitor progress and be aware. Set up procedures if you must. But remember that when you let your children assume responsibility for being self-starters, let them live with the aftereffects of their actions, too. They'll be the stronger for it.

And you'll discover a wonderful dividend: your relationship will be much more peaceful. After all, when you're constantly reminding and your child is always resisting, it's difficult for either of you to feel close and loving.

## Children Gain Confidence by Doing

One of the greatest gifts you can give your offspring is the freedom to try. Never do anything for your children that they can do for themselves. Remember when Matthew was beginning to put on his own clothes? His T-shirt went on inside out, his pants backwards, and his shoes on the wrong feet—and you laughed and said, "What a big boy!" That's how he learned to dress himself.

In the same way, encourage your children to keep stretching beyond what they've done before—and be supportive. Break new tasks into "baby steps" and expect some mistakes. That's part of the learning process. If Kara makes a poster for the 4-H bake sale, the printing will probably be less than perfect, but don't you do it over. Otherwise she won't try next time. It's more important that she acquire the joy of participating and feel proud rather than whether or not someone thinks her handiwork a bit messy.

Try to structure the environment of your home so that children can succeed. Then let them go to it! If Matthew wants to bake a cake, for instance, you wouldn't start him out with your from-scratch recipe for a three-layer white cake featuring grated fresh coconut. You'd give him a box of mix for a simple one-layer cake, and let him move up as he mastered techniques. When Kara wants to help paint, assign her to the backyard fence, not the living room wall. You want them to take on a challenge, but one they can handle. For if they feel overwhelmed or botch the job, they may quit trying.

Whenever you can, don't just specify chores for your youngsters, but work with them. And teach them how to carry out the task when they initially show curiosity, if possible.

"Some of my happiest childhood memories are of working in our huge garden with my mom," says Jim. "It always seemed easier to talk when we were hoeing or picking strawberries or down on our knees, pulling weeds. Somehow we never talked that way anyplace else. Mom's been gone a long time, but when I think of her, I think of us working out there in that garden together. And I treasure those times."

Nourish your children's learning with praise and be specific. For example, after Matthew's piano recital, you could compliment him, "You did very well!" That's good, but, "I was proud of the way you overcame your fear and smiled at the audience," is even better.

Tie your remarks to behavior rather than to the child's person. When Kara clears the dinner table without being asked, you might say, "Kara, you're such a good and helpful girl. Thank you!" Kara, however, may be thinking that yesterday she was anything but helpful and that today she took the dishes to the sink because she was feeling guilty. So your well-intended words don't register—and may even cause her to squirm inwardly. That's why it can be more beneficial to say, "Kara, I really appreciated you clearing the table while I was on the telephone. And it was especially nice because I didn't even ask you to!" That's honest praise she can accept and feel good about.

Phony praise accomplishes nothing and can even be destructive. After all, what incentive is there to improve if the same praise is given when the work is halfway completed as when one carries through? Self-respect and self-confidence grow from taking responsibility and performing tasks, yes, and affirmation reinforces good behavior. But not when the words are hypocritical. Such compliments reinforce bad habits.

It's a bit of a paradox. You want to applaud particular efforts, yet a major goal is that your children feel loved for who they are, not what they do. So concentrate on that of first importance: your love, given freely and without qualification. That's the cornerstone of your relationship, from the first day of your child's life.

## *The Family That Plays Together . . .*

Another way to help children feel loved and secure is to cultivate a sense of family. You can help establish that identification by developing family traditions for holidays and birthdays. Make them up as you go along, silly or elaborate. Blend in the best from your own (and your husband's) childhood(s). Then notice how your children

will proudly recite, "At *our* house we always . . ." Here are a few examples.
- The birthday person chooses the menu (or the restaurant).
- Set the birthday table with candles and your best china.
- Instead of birthday cards, compose original birthday poems and limericks.
- Wrap birthday gifts in brown paper or in the colorful Sunday comics.
- Hide birthday gifts and leave a treasure map.
- Leave only empty baskets and hide Easter eggs (indoors or out).
- Make homemade ice cream or have a watermelon feed on July 4; go watch the fireworks.
- Have a family movie night at the drive-in theater (when the film is suitable); bring along bags of homemade popcorn, apples, and a thermos of lemonade.
- Make home-baked breakfast rolls every weekend (even if they come from a can or box).
- At Thanksgiving, go around the table, and let each person share something for which they're thankful.
- Have an Advent wreath; light it for family devotions and let your amateur musicians "accompany" carol singing.
- Plan an annual family outing to cut the Christmas tree.
- String popcorn to decorate the tree.
- Assemble a Christmas box of food or playthings; leave it on the doorstep of a needy family (ring the doorbell and run—great fun for youngsters!).
- Tie small pre-Christmas gifts to the tree, to be opened at specified times.
- Instead of name tags, write clues and let the recipient guess what's inside before opening gifts.
- Fix "our food" each year on holidays (same pumpkin pie, same Christmas cookies, etc.).

Whatever they are, such traditions are another bit of glue for your mother-child bond. And one day your child will amaze you by asking, "You are going to make cranberries, aren't you? Thought I'd give them a try this year."

What about your day-to-day leisure time? Is it usually TV-after-supper at your house? True, TV is easy, and it's always available. But it doesn't reinforce your family togetherness. After all, whatever conversation there is will occur in spurts while the commercials are on. Consider setting one night a week aside for your family time—and make that the same priority as church and club meetings. Perhaps we could learn from some non-Christian religious sects, which make this a precept. For us it's optional, but there is a real strength in parents and children simply spending time and doing things together.

- Be creative and invest some effort in homegrown fun instead.
- Have an indoor picnic in January. Spread a blanket on the floor and serve picnic food. If you have a fireplace, roast hot dogs and marshmallows.
- Go biking or swimming or walk in the woods.
- Play board or card games that everyone can enjoy.
- Make up silly lyrics to well-known tunes.
- Get in the habit of singing in the car—kids love it!
- Put together a jigsaw puzzle.
- Have an informal rap session about a recent classroom learning or an item in the news. Does it conflict with the Christian faith? Does it have an impact or influence on your lives? (This is a great way to help youngsters, still in their formative years, to clarify thinking and apply their faith.)
- Make up a story that goes around the room; one person ends in the middle of a sentence, the next picking it up from there.
- Has anyone noticed a need in your community or church which you could work on together?
- Dream and plan together for your next vacation; set a money figure and let the children read background information, write to chambers of commerce about stops along the way, plan the route, etc.
- Work on family photo albums.
- Explore your public library, then read the books aloud.
- Plan and record newsy cassette tapes for faraway relatives.
- Bake cookies, make popcorn balls, etc.
- Each week appoint a "King/Queen for a Day" on a rotational basis; that person chooses the menu and after-dinner activities.

You're limited only by your imagination! But you don't always need planned activities. Surprises are often the most fun of all. So once in awhile be spontaneous. Forget about Saturday chores and delight in your child. Go for a walk; toss a ball; smell the flowers; lie on your backs under a tree and talk. It doesn't matter what you do—just make time to enjoy each other's company.

Shared family fun (and working together, as well) helps children realize that each is an essential part of the whole. The apostle Paul described each part of the body, each Christian as useful and needed (1 Cor. 12:4-5). So, too, is each family member. It's similar to a chemical formula. Each component is necessary and contributes a unique quality. Families are like that, too. As each child grows up and leaves home, you'll note that it feels as if a precious, indefinable element is missing, no matter how many remain.

So plan such mutual involvement now—strengthen your mother-child and sibling-sibling relationships. This pleasant companionship shores up the foundation of your life together, builds bridges of closeness, forms a reservoir of good will. The time and effort you invest now in building a team spirit will be money in the bank. The recollections will help you collectively ride out the storms of adolescence looming just off the horizon and bring you joy for a lifetime.

One other thing—learn to laugh more with your children. We parents are often so caught up with the seriousness and responsibility of our task that we go around with tight lips and a grim expression. After all, we must be ready to pounce so that we can pluck objectionable habits as soon as they sprout! (Perhaps if we laughed together more often there'd be less misbehavior.)

## Are You Real?

*D*on't be too proud to admit your mistakes. You won't ruin your credibility. Rather, as you acknowledge your own flaws, your offspring will love and respect you, because you'll be authentic. Or to put it into slang, "What you see is what you get!" Your children are also more likely to develop into open people who can confess, forgive, and accept others—because that's what they'll see in you. Part of being real is to model, not preach.

Our training of our children is, like the Father's training of you and me, rooted in our relationship. Within that context, we'll set guidelines for ourselves and our family. And like our heavenly Father, we won't equate giving love with giving approval. After all, we need His love most when we're most unlovable, most discouraged over our failures.

It's the same with us and our children. "Whenever I displeased my mother, a great gulf opened up between us," says Carla. "The atmosphere became positively frigid. She didn't talk to me except for 'Please pass the salt' or 'Don't forget your lunch.' I already felt bad enough—I didn't need that, too!"

Nobody does. Yet many adults grew up in homes where the style of parenting was even more destructive. If we're to keep such patterns from continuing, generation after generation, it will take continued effort. And continued prayer.

"I couldn't believe it," says Carla. "I was so positive that because I knew what had made me feel sad and unloved as a child, I'd never be like Mom. Then I had a child of my own and found that my natural, built-in reaction was to turn into an iceberg whenever Ashley acted up. Didn't even have to think about it—it was an instant feeling that just popped up, ready to go. If anyone asked what was wrong, I'd answer coldly, 'Oh, nothing. I just don't feel like talking.' My mother's very own words, coming out of *my* mouth! Once I realized what I was doing, I knew I had a choice. I could be a carbon copy of my mom or find a better way. It was up to me.

"I did a lot of praying!" Carla continues. "Even if I could change my actions, I didn't know how to change my feelings. The Lord somehow broke through all that, gradually. Now when Ashley disobeys, I deal with it. Then I give her a big hug and honestly tell her how much I love her. And that's that for both of us. We're free to go on. Our relationship doesn't suffer—and neither, thank God, does Ashley."

Our faithful God can overcome the negative programming we received as children. He can remake us from within, give us a new heart (2 Cor. 5:17), meet every need. Our Father loves us ... and we know it deep inside ourselves.

Our children need to know God's love as well as ours. That's why we worship and learn together as a family. That's why we naturally, gently, casually talk of God in ordinary conversation, sharing deeper insights as they grow and mature. For example, we tell our toddler, "God made the pretty flowers." With our grade-schoolers, we might say, "You're doing so well in school. Isn't it wonderful that God gives us the intelligence to learn?" With a three-year-old, we might say, "God made you and God made me. God loves you and God loves me." But when that child is nine, as we watch the TV news we could observe, "Did you ever think that God loves that beggar in India just as much as He loves you and me? After all, He made us all, and so we're all equal in His eyes."

Our goal is to impart heart knowledge, not head knowledge. Faith comes as a gift of the Holy Spirit, but we can nurture our children's relationship with their Savior. Grade-schoolers are old enough to understand many things, but are not yet cynical, so it's a receptive age at which to fortify that faith foundation.

To sum up, this is a time for building on the same principles we employed when our children were younger. We're generous with our unconditional love; we make few demands, but enforce those we make; we model forgiveness and restoration; we administer appropriate punishment with restraint and tact; we avoid inconsiderate and destructive talk; we realize that our child's concept of God will be highly influenced by what they observe in us; we're liberal with praise, affirmation, and touching because we know that our children's self-image and security largely comes from what they *think* we think of them.

That's a tall order, fellow parents! But our God is faithful, and He has promised to supply all our needs as we bring them before Him (Phil. 4:19). Grade-school-age children are perhaps in the best years of childhood. They no longer need the close supervision and personal care of earlier years, and they're not yet in the Terrible Teens. A word to the wise: enjoy them while it lasts!

**For Further Reading:**

Braga, Joseph and Laurie. *Children and Adults: Activities for Growing Together*. Prentice-Hall, 1976. Activities for parents to do with children;

most are low cost; many explore feelings; book includes homemade toys and word games.

Campbell, D. Ross, M.D. *How to Really Love Your Child,* Victor Books, 1977. Christian-oriented; practical advice on conveying the love you feel, including loving discipline.

Gaither, Gloria and Shirley Dobson. *Let's Make a Memory.* Word Books, 1983. Christian-oriented resource book that will help foster family traditions; contains many creative suggestions and activities for holidays and special occasions.

Gaulke, Earl H. *You Can Have a Family Where Everybody Wins.* Concordia, 1975. Christian perspective on Parent Effectiveness Training; excellent communication techniques; good tie-in with Scriptural principles.

Ginott, Dr. Haim G. *Between Parent and Child.* MacMillan, 1965. Good examples of communication techniques with children; can seem tedious at times, but has good insights.

Hendricks, Howard G. *Heaven Help the Home!* Victor Books, 1974. Christian-oriented; easy reading; principles for successful family living.

# 4

# "Really, Mother!"

## The Wonderful, Baffling Adolescent

*A mother is not a person to lean on
but a person to make leaning unnecessary.*
      *Dorothy Canfield Fisher*

*Don't laugh at a youth for his affectations;
he's only trying on one face after another
till he finds his own.*
      *Logan Pearsall Smith*

*Parents need to fill a child's bucket
of self-esteem so high that the rest
of the world can't poke enough holes
in it to drain it dry.*
      *Alvin Price*

*Oh, to be only half as wonderful
as my child thought I was when he was small,
and only half as stupid
as my teenager now thinks I am.*
      *Rebecca Richards*

What do you think of when you hear the word *teenager*?

Some parents see it in giant, flashing neon lights. You can hear it in their conversation.

"I'm scared silly! Next year she'll be a TEENAGER!"

"I don't know if I have what it takes to survive his TEENAGE years!"

"TEENAGERS today are so much brighter than we were. I don't know how to *talk* to my kids!"

"She was such a darling—until she became a TEENAGER. Now we can't communicate at all!"

"My TEENAGER is driving me nuts!"

"Enjoy your little ones, my dear. Before you know it, they'll be TEENAGERS—and it will be war!"

So let's get something straight at the beginning. A teenager is simply a more complex version of a grade-schooler—who was a more complex version of a toddler. So don't be intimidated!

This is the same child you've loved and cared for since birth, with the same basic needs of a year or two ago. Only now your youngster is in a period of transition, no longer a child, yet not an adult, either. (That explains the sudden flip-flops back and forth; for instance, one minute a teen will offer an opinion that's remarkably insightful and mature, and then in the next sentence sound like a whiny three-year-old.)

For some the mysterious emotional process that necessarily, it seems, marks the passage from child to adult, begins at age 11 or 12. For others it starts at 13 or 14. A few wait until they're past 16 years old. And when it ends is just as variable. (The accompanying physical changes don't necessarily follow an identical timetable.)

Your teenagers, let's call them Christy and Brent, need your genuine love and acceptance as much now as they ever did—perhaps more. Yet they may not acknowledge what you say or do, may appear uncaring, alienated. Don't let them fool you! Brent and Christy crave your listening ear, even though they may seem to shun conversation and don't seem to hear you. They need your presence, although they may seem to avoid you.

Your teens yearn for your support—although they'll

reject your advice;
take your generosity for granted;
make a face when you praise them; and
make it plain that they'd rather be with their friends.

Believe it or not, this contradiction has a logical explanation. A major factor in this developmental process is the young person's inward imperative to cut the emotional ties with parents. Paradoxically, the more attached the adolescent feels to the parents, the more tempestuous the break may be. That's because your young person identifies so closely with you that he or she may feel the only way to achieve autonomy of thought and emotion is to make a complete break.

As one counselor put it, "They have to hate you before they can love you." Adolescents must withdraw from their parents in order to decide their own values and preferences, to sort out their own feelings. They want to become—in their own eyes—separate persons. They'll "return" when they feel secure within themselves and have decided, "This is how *I* feel, not how Mom or Dad thinks I should feel."

That's probably how teenagers earned their reputation for being contrary. You know how it goes: if parents approve, they won't want it, whatever it is. Keep the foregoing explanation in mind, and you'll understand why if you say to Christy, "I think you look super in that blue sweater," she'll likely choose the purple instead. If you tell Brent that you think his best friend's hair style is atrocious, count on seeing its copy adorning your son's head in a few weeks.

Christy and Brent are, in a word, normal—for teenagers. Each, you see, is proving their independence of thought. At this point they're out to demonstrate to the world (and especially to you!) that they're not simply extensions of you. Consider their assignment through their eyes and such behavior seems logical.

You may be tempted to try manipulating them by reverse psychology. For example, "I don't want Christy to date Jon, so I'll pour on the compliments about how good-looking he is, how much I like him, and so forth. Then she probably won't go near him!" Uh-uh. Your teenagers know the real you. You won't fool them for long. Eventually, they'll resent your maneuvering and respect you less.

Your most constructive approach is to allow them to be different, even outlandish, at least in minor matters. If Brent wants to dress in old army fatigues, don't say a word—unless it's against school policy. If Christy insists on "Magnificent Magenta" lips and "Overheated Orange" fingernails, swallow your comments. Either she's "in" and her friends will adore the look (in which case your comments mean nothing). Or else they'll let her know she looks ridiculous, and she'll never sport that combination again.

Remember, your goal is to maintain a strong relationship with your child. So, as the saying goes, "Don't sweat the small stuff." Save your confrontations for situations that are important enough to be worth it. And know that, if you draw a line and challenge your teenager not to cross it "or else," you'll have to live with the consequences. Can you?

Parents of teenagers have a choice. You can relax and place some confidence in your young people, even though they may appear to have discarded your values (provided, of course, that their health and personal safety won't be affected). Or you can resist their fledgling attempts to be independent persons and seek to retain close control. If you choose the latter course, they'll likely become increasingly determined and openly defiant. Or they'll give up and retreat within themselves.

That doesn't mean that you never speak up, that you let teenagers do as they please. Do communicate your standards, offer your opinions, but quietly, reasonably—and not repetitiously. Stand your ground when you feel it's vital, for instance, your commitment to worshiping the Lord together as a family. And never be afraid to say no. Although adolescents rail against authority and family rules, they need them—want them. Your loving limits are their security blanket, their assurance that you care.

One more thing: see that your teens are well-grounded in the Christian faith. Like us, they need a standard by which to live. Begin with God's "guardrails" for living (Ex. 20:1-17; Matt. 22:36-40; John 14:15, 23-24). Each of us needs to recognize the absolute standard of almighty God and our own inability to walk that narrow path. Only then will we truly appreciate what Jesus Christ did for us on the cross (Rom. 5:8; Gal. 3:10-13; 1 John 1:5-10; 2:1-2; 5:11-12).

Since your teens continually face strong temptation, it's also vital that they realize Christ's death and resurrection frees us, but doesn't impart license to sin (Rom. 6). True, we *are* forgiven! He *will* strengthen us in temptation (1 Cor. 10-13; Heb. 2:14). Nevertheless, Jesus also expects His followers to stand out from the world around (Matt. 5—7). An impossible challenge! Yet He has also promised to indwell us and empower us for living (John 14:16-20, 27; 2 Cor. 5:17; 1 John 4:4).

First, last, and forever, impress on your young people the endless mercy of God (Ps. 86:5-7, 15; 103:8-14; 106:1). Otherwise they may become overwhelmed by their failures. They desperately need the continuing deep assurance of God's presence and abiding love, as well as knowledge of Christ's gift of eternal life (Ps. 42:8; John 3:16; 2 Tim. 2:19). The resulting inner peace will help guide them surely and safely along the thorny road marked Teenage Years.

And don't label *every* departure from *your* norm as a rebellion. Don't turn *every* difference of opinion into a standoff in which you must prove that you're right, that you have the clout. You well may win the battle and lose your child—or at least cause your teenager to despair of ever getting through to you. Many adolescents complain, "My parents never really listen to me." And they're right!

What teens long for is summed up in their battle cry, "Give me some space!" Translation:

Don't hold on so tightly.
Let me grow up.
Let me figure out who I am and don't be threatened when I have a different opinion.
Love me even when I'm not what you want me to be.
Respect me as a person with potential.
Give me some time to find my way.
Allow me to be me, a person separate from you.

If you analyze that point of view, you'll find that it's very similar to what *we* desire from other adults who love us and are important to us. We, too, want room to grow, acceptance as we are, support that continues even if *we* are, at times, a disappointment.

## *Do Less Talking—More Listening*

Your most important task right now is to keep the lines of communication open between you and your adolescent. That means that you do more listening than talking. You don't jump right in and pronounce judgment. You don't ridicule or label your child—or your child's friends. You seek to preserve and to strengthen your young person's self-image. (And if you remember your own teen years, you'll know how desperately that's needed.) You seek to discern emotions, not just to hear words. You don't force conversations, but at the same time, you pick up on logical openings.

For example, when Christy tells you about the girl in her class who's pregnant, stifle your immediate 30-minute lecture. Be relaxed and let her talk. Don't be afraid of silences, because on sensitive issues it often takes time for young persons to work up the courage to share their thoughts. Gently draw her out. Eventually you may be able to lead the discussion around to the pain that can result from sexual relations between unmarried persons, especially teens. That's a natural lead-in to reaffirming God's standards and talking about how our Christian faith relates to everyday living. You may feel uncomfortable. If so, be honest: "I feel a bit strange—kind of inadequate—talking with you about sex" (or any particular subject). Your teen may reply, "Me, too!" and then you're on your way. Your aim is a two-way discussion, not a parental monologue.

When Brent tells you that he's thinking of dropping out of school, don't pounce and preach. Rather, listen for the feelings. Let him talk. What are his frustrations, his fears? Be sure to convey that you love him as before and that you'll always be proud of him, no matter what. *Then* you can examine the various options (and attendant consequences) and help him work it through. Chances are that he just needs to ventilate his uncertainties.

Listen with openness and acceptance. Communicate your love and support. Try to relate not as a paragon but as a fellow redeemed (yet still sinful) human being, who also thoughtfully struggles to live by Christian values. Then your teens will feel comfortable bringing their concerns to you. Young people, after all, *need* parents. Be a parent, however, who's a reassuring friend.

There will be times when you'll have to fight back the words—your fears, your admonishments, your anger. And certainly you need to be honest about your feelings, because teenagers can smell phoniness, and it makes them sick. Just don't leap in with on-the-spot judgments and pronouncements. *Really listen!* They need to feel it's safe to share with you what's going on with them and their friends, or they'll seek advice, instead, from their peers. Then you'll not only be on the outside but you'll lose the chance to be a sounding board or to offer a word of counsel. They'll never tell you *everything*— don't expect them to. Still, prove yourself a wise, calm, trustworthy confidant, and you'll enjoy a relationship with your young person that most other mothers long for.

## Can't Talk? Try Writing It Down

**P**erhaps you're thinking, "Easy for you to talk! My teenager and I can't seem to carry on a civil conversation, no matter how hard I try. And I guess he tries, too. Yet before I know what's happening, one of us is yelling."

That's not an unusual situation. Or sometimes there's a particular subject you feel you can't discuss. You're sure you won't be able to get through the conversation without getting weepy and as a result won't be able to make your point. Or you might be sure your young person will interrupt you before you've expressed your thought— maybe even slam out of the room in a temper.

Some parents find it very satisfactory at times to communicate via notes. Sure, talking it over is better. But exchanging notes beats letting feelings fester and grow.

"My Consuelo and I only passed paper between us for maybe a month," says Rosa. "See, she's mad all the time. And I've got one hot temper myself! Every time we try to talk, boom! We're blowing up! One morning after she leaves for school, I walk into the bathroom, and it's a disaster—again. Wet towels, dirty tub, bottles everywhere. What makes me super angry is the nail polish spilled on the counter. Good thing she was gone—I was really ticked off!

"Well, I can't get at her until after school, and I have to go to work, anyhow. So I leave her the mess and a long note telling her how I feel and that it better be cleaned up when I get home. It works! The place is shiny! She even washes the towels! So I think, hey, maybe I've got something here!

"By then she's gone, so I leave her another note, telling her how good everything looks, and I go to bed. Next morning *I* find a note," Rosa continues. "Will I please think about letting her go to the school party with a boy? So I think it over and decide maybe it's time, so I tape a yes note to the mirror before I go to work. When I get home there's a thank-you note from Consuelo, and she says she loves me!

"First time I hear that in a long time! Makes me feel so good I start leaving notes every now and then, good stuff as well as when I'm ready to blow. And I try to remember to tell her that I love her, either way. So that's how we make it through," says Rosa. "Saves us from a lot of big hassles! Now Consuelo's herself again, and we talk all the time. Funny thing . . . I kinda miss those notes."

For note writers the same guidelines apply as in conversation with your teens.

- State the facts, don't accuse. ("The bathroom looks like a bomb hit it," rather than, "When will you ever learn to clean up after yourself? Do you have to be such a slob?")
- Tell how you feel in "I" messages. ("When *I* saw the bathroom in a mess, *I* felt really angry," not, "You make me so angry when you leave your things all over the bathroom every time you use it.")
- Stick to the issue. ("Everyone who uses the bathroom is responsible for cleaning up after themselves," rather than, "Today it's the bathroom, yesterday you forgot to call, and a person can't even walk through your bedroom.")
- Be specific about what you expect, without threats. ("I expect the bathroom to be cleaned up when I get home—and to stay clean from now on," not, "If you don't shape up around here, pretty soon you're going to be in a lot of trouble!")
- Always affirm your love. (They probably won't respond, may not even believe it at the time, but they like to read—hear—it nevertheless.)

## Keep Out—This Means You

*I*f you haven't learned it before, this is the time to take it seriously:

adolescents prize privacy and deeply resent parents poking around in their domain. It doesn't matter that they've nothing to hide. It's a key factor in their crusade for autonomy. So *always* knock before entering. Until you're invited in, stay out of their rooms. Leave the cleanup detail to them. Let Christy straighten out her own dresser drawers. Leave Brent's freshly laundered underwear in a pile on the dryer or outside his bedroom door.

Of course, you'd never read diaries or open mail addressed to your teens. But you want your teenagers to know without any doubt that you wouldn't even read an opened letter they left lying on the kitchen counter or listen in on the extension phone. Some parents think that they need to keep tabs on what goes on in their children's lives. Mom goes in to vacuum Christy's room and "just happens" to read an upsetting note from her girlfriend Amanda. She straightens out Brent's things and "accidentally" discovers a pack of cigarettes. When one of their friends calls, Mother stays close by. Once in awhile she picks up the bedroom extension "by mistake"—and listens in.

Yes, you want to be aware, but such tactics don't solve problems. They only create new ones. What happens? Brent and Christy feel betrayed, spied upon. So, logically, they go underground. Christy will continue to see Amanda, but she won't mention it—and she'll discard any notes in the corner trash can. Brent will still try out cigarettes, only now he'll stash them elsewhere. In other words, they'll turn to deception if that's the only way they can maintain privacy. They'll watch their words v-e-r-y carefully—and you probably won't find any more "incriminating evidence." All will be well—on the surface. But you'll have dealt your mother-child relationship a deadly blow.

This is *not* meant to imply that you drop your standards or remove all parental constraints! There will be times when you must say, "Look, I trust you, but I don't think you have the experience yet to make this judgment. So this time we have to do it my way." That approach is not a personal putdown, and your teen will likely accept it more-or-less gracefully. And of course, you should state how you feel about smoking—or anything else. But do so in a reasonable manner and don't become a broken record, stuck in the same old groove, playing the same line over and over again. Do make an effort to find out who your children's friends are and to get acquainted, but avoid continual checking and questioning.

The point is that your teenagers see their No. 1 purpose in life as becoming independent. And to them that means choosing their own friends, deciding their values, and protecting their privacy. So if you seem to be interfering with that process, no matter how loving and well-intentioned you are, they'll almost certainly just become more determined. They know (and you fear) that when they're out of your sight, you lose control.

As with everything else in life, they learn and grow by experience. Prevent them from assuming increasing responsibility for self-government and their character will remain flabby, unable to support itself. So at whatever age you're no longer in the picture, the young person must *then* learn to cope, to say no, to make judgments, and to adopt a set of personal standards. (That explains why young people from apparently exemplary Christian homes sometimes "fall apart" when they go off to college. For the first time in their lives they have the opportunity to make their own decisions. They may be old enough to vote, yet be infants when it comes to the development of their inner control.)

Far better to simply trust them. Risky? Perhaps. And in some situations more than others. But do parents really have any other choice? We can fight it, block it, rage against it. Or we can accept it gracefully. Either way, it's an inevitable fact that we can't be with our teenagers every minute of every day, and they *will* grow up and away from us. Allowing them to have privacy removes the need for them to leave home or to sneak around in order to escape prying eyes and eavesdropping ears. We aim to send out into the world young adults who are strong and vigorous in spirit as well as mind and body. That comes from learning to exercise self-government.

Besides, a sturdy mother-child relationship is built on trust—and that goes both ways.

## *Environmental Concerns*

*I*n the interest of your own mental health, make your teenagers responsible for the cleanup of their individual bedrooms. Try to ignore the condition in between.

"My good friend Miranda is a child psychologist," says Ruby. "My Erin was 11 or 12 when Miranda advised me to stay out of Erin's room and not to get upset when it looked like the city dump. She said that kids feel they're being nagged at *all* the time, that they need a place that's theirs alone, where nobody will bother them. Miranda said, 'Shut the door to Erin's room and pretend it doesn't belong to the house anymore.' Thought that was the dumbest thing I ever heard, but she's the expert, so I gave it a try.

"Told Erin she had to look at her bedroom, so it was up to her to keep it clean. Keeping my lip zipped was the killer, but I stuck with it. Sometimes I'd get up the courage to take a peek, then wished I hadn't. That place would be knee-deep in litter! When I couldn't stand it anymore, I'd tell Erin to clean it up, and she would, moaning and groaning all the while. And it would stay neat an hour or two.

"Anyhow, that's the way it went while Erin was in high school. But guess what!" Ruby continues. "When she got into her own place, Erin suddenly turned into Mrs. Clean! She can't even stand a dirty coffee mug sitting in the sink overnight!" Now our younger daughter, Kelley, is in seventh grade," says Ruby, rolling her eyes. "I can see the cycle starting all over again. I just keep telling myself that one day it will all be over . . ."

True. In fact, there's one handy-dandy motto that fits every stage of parenting: This, too, shall pass.

## *Raising Responsible Teens*

*T*he authorities agree: the wise mother aims to work herself out of a job. Simply put, that means that all through your children's growing-up years you gradually let them assume more and more responsibility for themselves. Underline that in red for the teenage years! Now's the time to let them try—and perhaps fail—because you're still around to lend a hand if it's needed.

Like the rest of us, teens learn best from personal experience. If Christy throws her favorite angora sweater in the washer and it comes out toddler-size, it's unfortunate. But it's a cinch that she'll then be more ready to learn your good laundry techniques. (And what does she learn if you always carefully hand launder her things?) If Brent is down to 25 cents a week before next payday, at least he'll eat at your table while he contemplates the benefits of budgeting. (If you bail him out, what does he learn?)

Again, it's a sort of tough love, of letting our almost-grownup offspring learn from the natural consequences of their actions. With teenagers, we parents are naturally apprehensive about that idea. Their dangers are more serious, seemingly more urgent—and the "natural consequences" not a bit to our liking. Nevertheless, it's time to begin handing over control.

One mother who saw her children pass through adolescence safe and sound—and emerge on the other side as dependable young adults—offers these guidelines which worked in her family.

1. When your children reach the age of 13 or thereabouts, put them on an allowance to cover clothing, school lunches and expenses, personal items, etc. Set out the ground rules clearly and be sure everyone understands:

    a. First priority: regular church contributions.

    b. No borrowing or advances (except in real emergencies). If you run out of money, you'll have to make do until next payday, just like everyone else.

    c. Clothing purchases are your choice, but you'll need an okay on major items, such as winter coats.

    d. So long as your clothing choices are not indecent and will be acceptable at school, I won't interfere or criticize. (Note to mothers: Be prepared to live with some weird outfits, but keep your word.)

    e. If you buy clothing that requires dry cleaning or other special care, you provide it.

    f. You can buy your lunch or pack it from home. However, you cannot skip lunch just to save money or time.

2. You're now responsible for your own washing and ironing. I'll be glad to answer questions or demonstrate. (Note to mothers: This saves arguments over how many times per day a sane person changes clothes.)

3. Write your after-school and weekend schedule on the family

calendar, with a phone contact if possible. Call me, if you're going to be late—and I'll do the same.

4. (For families where more than one driver uses the same car) Note the times you need the car on the calendar. In general, the first one to reserve the car gets it, although parents have first priority. (Note to mothers: You'll have to work out in advance how you'll handle gas cost.)

What does all this have to do with the mother-child bond? Simply this: Adolescents complain, "Nobody listens to me. People snoop into my things. They treat me like a baby! It's *my* life—why can't I make my own decisions? And why are my folks so stingy with money?"

These are five areas that commonly cause repeated squabbles. So isn't it logical to assume that if these trouble areas are resolved, your relationship with your children will be strengthened? Wouldn't you feel warmer toward them if they didn't complain so much? They'll speedily discover that such self-determination isn't an automatic end to their problems. But if the decisions are their own, they have no one else to blame, so there's not much point in grumbling.

## *Hard Questions*

This giving up control goes beyond everyday routines, where the answers may seem fairly clear-cut. Many situations that arise through your children's teenage years are difficult. You examine the factors from all sides and find that, rather than black-and-white, there are many shades of gray to the possible answers.

For example, Christy's good friend Jolene lives with her divorced father. Jolene seems like a nice girl, but Mother is uneasy because Christy is spending "too much" time at that home. Christy counters that at least Jolene doesn't have little brothers and a nosey sister all over the place, so the two girls can talk in peace. Mother has spoken with Mr. Jones, and he seems a well-balanced, loving father, so she wonders whether she's being silly. Yet Bill Jones *is* athletic and good-looking . . .

Brent is determined to go out for football, and mother is white with fear. She remembers a schoolmate who was paralyzed for life at the age of 17 because of a football injury . . .

Mom insists that Christy take bookkeeping, knowing it will be a usable skill for a lifetime. Yet Christy finally made first chair in the clarinet section, and band is scheduled for the same class period . . . Because he's bright and has a natural aptitude for math, either engineering or something in computers seems a wise choice for a career. Brent, however, wants to be a mechanic and insists he doesn't need college prep courses . . .

Jobs are hard to find, but Christy can get one nights and weekends at the local drive-in. Mom doesn't like the hours or the location, but the money would certainly be welcome . . .

Since Brent started dating Kim a year ago, he seems to think of nothing else. Kim, a sexy little number, is "all over Brent," no matter where they are. His part-time job keeps him too busy to date much, but they're on the phone constantly. Brent's longtime dream was to be a veterinarian, and he made good grades. Now he doesn't seem to care . . .

What's a parent to do? There are no pat answers. Each situation must be evaluated individually—and sometimes the answer isn't completely satisfying to anyone. It's never easy for parents to watch helplessly while our children "ruin their lives"—at least in our opinion. In the early teens it's easier to exert parental control. Choices aren't usually so threatening to the young person's future. That comes later.

In any case, you'll try to have a reasonable discussion first. (In fact, you'll probably have several!) But after laying out all your arguments for or against, you may be stymied. You could impose new restraints—for awhile. Yet there comes a time when your children must make their own decisions. Their own mistakes. They *will* live their own lives, with or without your approval.

So the important thing is to keep your mutual love alive and intact. Many a sorrowing parent remembers saying, "If you _____ (fill in the blanks), don't come crying to me when it all falls apart!"

And the child lives up to that bargain. The bridges are burned. The river of love dries up. The parent ("I make the rules around here, and I'm gonna prove who's boss!") is left alone. And lonely.

You don't want that. So let's be realistic. As business people say, let's take a "worst-case position." What's the worst thing that could happen?

To watch your offspring make decisions, especially if you suspect they're being foolhardy, is frightening. When your young person is self-supporting and of legal age, however, he or she has the right to make unwise choices. (And not all wait for those milestones before doing so.)

This young person could, indeed, make a serious mistake. The results could be disastrous—excruciatingly painful to all concerned. Months or even years of your beloved child's life could be wasted or damaged. But as long as your young person is *alive*, as long as your relationship endures, both of you can go on!

If (when) the dream shatters, welcome your prodigal back to your arms and kill the fatted calf. Then celebrate second chances and learning and the depth human beings gain through hurt and heartache. One day you'll see some good from it (Rom. 8:28). (And *never* say, "I told you so!")

In talking over such hard questions and differences of opinions, you'll find far less strain if you've made time for talking things over all along. One way is to deliberately create opportunities for you to be alone with your teenager. You might schedule a lunch or dinner together at a restaurant (or some fast food establishment) every month or oftener. (Though you certainly want to talk more than once a month!) Get tickets for a sporting event, a concert, a good movie when you can find one. Some parents take a child along on occasional short business trips, the young person enjoying the swimming pool or going exploring while the parent is in meetings. Or plan an overnight trip to a nearby city and go together to the tourist attractions.

Utilize the built-in openings, too. For example, you may be driving your teenager to and from various lessons and school activities. That can give you time to talk. Once in awhile stop for a hamburger or an ice cream soda. (Leave a casserole in the oven for the rest of the family.) Be alert, too, for those times when everyone is gone but you and your teenager. Don't let such moments slip by you—use them to keep your communication alive and comfortable.

Mealtimes provide another opportunity to keep in touch. But

having the clan leisurely gathered around the dinner table may be mostly a memory, what with teenagers, now more mobile, rushing off to the library and play practice and basketball games. So think about family breakfasts. That's often the only time of the day when everyone is in the house at the same time!

It will, as usual, be mostly up to you because you'll probably be in charge—at least of getting it organized. And if your family has been in the habit of skipping breakfast altogether or of grabbing something on the run, everyone will have to get up a bit earlier.

But it's worth the effort! You'll start off the day with a bolstered feeling of family. You'll have a chance to discuss the coming day's scheduled activities. And if Brent is uneasy about a test or Dad faces a business challenge or you have a taxing day ahead, you can encourage each other. Best of all you'll have a natural opening for centering on God. You might want to begin with a psalm or with a few verses of Scripture, then allow time for off-the-cuff sentence prayers. At first you may be the only one praying, but don't give up. Your children will hear you commit their day to the Lord, as well as your own. That's a faith-strengthening thing in itself. Keep at it, without nagging or pleading, and one day someone else will join in.

Don't try for a long family devotion. Keep it brief and down-to-earth. But try it! This can grow into a precious family tradition, even though your loved ones may be lukewarm at first.

## Parents Can Have Identity Crises, Too!

**E**veryone knows that adolescence is an up-and-down time for the developing child. But realize that you, too, may be in an "awkward age." Consider the recent changes in your own life.

- Your teenager, given a choice, would usually opt for the peer group. In fact, it often seems as if your teen is deliberately avoiding being around you.
- You're no longer "the authority." Especially if your teenager is female, you probably haven't worn the right clothes or makeup or hairstyle for years. Nor do you know how to talk or decorate your home—and your views are hopelessly out-of-date. In short, you can't do anything quite right! (How long this stage lasts will vary,

but it's an almost universal disease. Just remember that teenagers are in the process of differentiating themselves from their parents. So you'll never be "right" for very long—and they'll let you know it! At this stage adolescents are mostly wrapped up in themselves. Their thoughtless comments, though normal, can still hurt. But don't take such remarks to heart and brood about them. Accept them as a typical manifestation of the species and develop selective hearing.)

- Your adolescents are beginning to exert their own authority. For years you've held the power; now they want it for themselves.
- Teens frequently appear to espouse different values from your own. Your formerly clean-cut son may adopt a clothing style and a manner you consider absurd. Your daughter may be involved with questionable friends. They're not interested (nor moved) by your opinions.
- Whereas once your children valued your views, now they may ridicule you for being narrow-minded or behind-the-times.

These—and other—factors add up to rejection. No human being likes that, not even a mother. It's hard on one's ego and self-esteem. Knowing that it's a natural part of growth doesn't remove the sting. Nor does it help that your teenager may be a walking, breathing example of what you *used* to be.

"I finally figured out why I was struggling," says Marilyn. "It hit me one day when Lisa was prancing around in her new jeans which, of course, fit her like wallpaper. I looked at those tiny little hips and realized I hadn't been that size since I was in fifth grade! Then I watched her with her boyfriend. You could feel the spark between them! I remember when Gary and I were like that. When we were first married, we couldn't get enough of each other. But now . . ."

(Gary, by the way, looks at son Tim, who's three inches taller and 30 pounds lighter—all muscle. Then he catches a glimpse of his own silhouette in the mirror and is startled to observe that his own pot belly is a carbon copy of his father's . . .)

Our young people remind us, too, that we're no longer kids ourselves, that we are, indeed, moving into middle age. But don't fall into the trap of trying to relive your youth by dressing or talking like a teenager. Michelle's mother did that. "Mom's little and blonde and about a size five—and there for awhile she dressed like she was 15, not 38!" says Michelle. "Everytime my friends were at the house, there was Mom, the center of attention, talking all the time! And there I was, feeling left out. She'd even flirt a little with the guys. It's really hard when your own mother is your competition!"

We can never truly be one of the young crowd again, nor should we try. We'll probably just end up looking a bit silly and embarrassing our own teenagers. So the message is this: be a mother who's a friend, not a friend who's a mother.

Perhaps one reason it's tempting to try to retrieve our youth is because somebody changed the signals in the middle of our lives. "I envy my children," Marilyn continues. "Take Lisa—she has so many options. Today a woman can do anything! She has her whole future ahead of her—and a lot of mine is already used up. Lisa wants to work in the space program. Women hadn't even thought of that when I was a teenager. Makes me feel ancient! I know I probably have a lot of years left. Just the same, I'm limited in my choices because of decisions I made when I was younger. My life has been good, but sometimes I wish I had another whack at deciding how to spend it. Some things just aren't possible anymore!"

That's life, true. But that's also the explanation for the unsettledness that may be churning around below *your* exterior. Some parents recognize it and then feel silly about those thoughts. They're the lucky ones, because perceiving our emotions is a necessary first step to working them through. Many other parents don't (or can't) admit those feelings.

All sorts of ambivalent emotions may surface, causing you to wonder, "What's gotten into me, anyhow?" Answer: Nothing. You're normal. Parents, as well as adolescents, sometimes struggle to find out who they are. Be kind to yourself. You're "just going through a stage."

Learn to be secure within yourself instead of depending on your teens for approval. Do you see yourself objectively? Take time to write down your own good qualities—what you like about yourself. Post the list where you can refer to it easily—as on your bathroom mirror. Some days that will be your only affirmation, so keep it handy.

Build your teenager's self-esteem, yes, but strengthen your own, as well. Be yourself. Choose clothes that make *you* feel good, for example. Young people want parents to be up-to-date, but don't attempt to look or to sound like one of their crowd. A teenager wants a mother who looks and acts and talks like a mother. (That doesn't imply "matronly," but rather a mature, self-assured woman.)

By the way, if you and your teens exhibit few or none of the foregoing behaviors and emotions, don't decide there must be something wrong with you! Some parents and children seem to pass through these years smoothly, and never is heard a discouraging word. (And the skies are not cloudy all day.) It depends a lot on individual temperaments, as well as on your relationship. If you're a mother and teenager like that, shout "Hallelujah!" and count your blessings!

## *Testing Your Mettle*

*I*f by now you're getting the idea that parenting one's children through the adolescent years can be a challenge, you're categorically correct. Obviously it takes maximum patience, probably more than you ever dreamed you possessed. But if you're to be the kind of mother you want to be (and if you didn't aim to reach your fullest potential, you wouldn't bother reading books like this), you'll also find several other qualities beneficial.

*Sensitivity.* Learn when to speak, when to be silent, when to give an extra hug (Eccl. 3:4, 5, 7). If you make it your business to be aware, you'll intuitively sense when to back off and when your teens need you to "be there for them." Learn to discern which is which—and don't nurse hurt feelings if they want to cope alone (Col. 3:12-14).

*Empathy.* Look at *their* world, through *their* eyes. Feel with them, not just for them (Rom. 12:15; Gal. 6:2).

*Positive expectations.* Remember that children tend to live out what parents expect of them—good or bad. So avoid the destructive (and untrue!) assumption that "all kids are on drugs; all teenagers are sexually active; all teens are on their way to becoming alcoholics;" and the like. Rather, *expect* your adolescents to be fine young people who are on the way to becoming exceptional young adults. Compliment them on what they do right, rather than always pointing out what they do wrong. The apostle Paul gives us the standard in Phil. 4:4-9.

*Love that shows.* See them as they are and love them anyway. Leave no doubt that your love for your offspring does not vary—that you attach no ifs, and, buts or, whens to it (John 13:34-35; Eph. 5:2; 1 John 4:7-11).

*Strength.* Be the steadying influence, the shoulder to cry on, the calm, mature grownup (Rom. 15:1-2). Know where to go to find your own strength (Is. 40:29-31; Phil. 4:13).

*Genuineness.* Don't be afraid to laugh with your teenagers, cry with them. Share your honest emotions and concerns. This isn't weakness. Rather, it's a chance to exemplify an important object lesson: adults, even Christian adults, also experience fear and disappointment and sorrow. But they're not destroyed; they don't lose their perspective or reason for living. Mature Christians seek God's guidance, then face the situation, work it through, and go on. Young people need to glimpse the pain so that they can recognize the gain in faith lived out (Ps. 37:23-24; 40:1-3; 1 Cor. 10:13; 2 Cor. 1:3-4).

*Honesty and openness* (Eph. 4:25). You won't blow your image if your teens know you made a mistake. Admit it. You won't lessen your authority if you apologize. Don't be afraid to expose your own failures and needs, either. For instance, instead of just saying, "I'm praying that you'll have the strength to overcome," you might say, "You need to quit wasting time and to buckle down in your studies. I need to quit smoking. Let's make a deal. I'll pray for you, and you pray for me. Let's take God at His Word and count on Him to strengthen us both." Then you become partners in each other's success, not adversaries.

More than we realize, our children see us as we really are. So who do we think we're kidding? When we have the courage to be transparent, they're more able to approach us with their own struggles and failures. If they observe that we persevere because we depend on our faithful God to forgive, sustain, and comfort us, the Christian faith comes alive. That's a difficult concept to convey—it's best experienced or witnessed firsthand.

*Confidentiality.* When your young person shares hopes and

hurts, don't broadcast them. *Never* betray your children's confidence! Speak well of your children to their friends—and to your own, as well. Teens are devastated when someone says, "Your mom's been telling my mom all about . . ." (Ps. 141:3; Rom. 14:19; Eph. 4:29).

*Strong principles.* Stand for something! Don't talk it and lecture it—put your money where your mouth is. Prove the truth of your advertised values by your life. At times your teens may appear headed in another direction, may even ridicule your standards. Nevertheless, you are their most influential day-in, day-out role model. You are the tree near which the apple will eventually come to rest (Rom. 12:2; Eph. 4:1-6, 22-32).

It's important, however, to be sensitive as well. Do you always have to prove that you're right? Is it vitally important that you "win," even if your child is humiliated in the process?

*Relinquishment.* Learn to let go of the reins (Eccl. 3:2, 6). Let your adolescents assume more and more responsibility for themselves, increasingly make their own choices, learn by doing. The principle is that along with each new freedom goes greater accountability. Award that opportunity now, while you're still available as a back-up, rescuer, or banker. Be ready to entrust them to our faithful God (Ps. 37:25-26; 103:17).

*Humility,* judiciously seasoned with assertiveness. Don't be domineering (1 Cor. 13:4; Eph. 4:2), but don't be a doormat, either (2 Tim. 1:7).

*Sense of humor.* This will enable you to laugh more, cry less (Prov. 17:22).

*Self-confidence.* Aim for the assurance that's sturdy enough to withstand the badgering of adolescents, who are often thoughtless and inconsiderate. Remember who you are—and whose you are. Look at your image in the mirror and repeat to yourself: Rom. 8:15; Eph. 5:1-2; Col. 2:6-7.

*Forgiveness.* Yes, your children will hurt you and disappoint you—many times. They, like you, are sinners. Pass on what *you* have received from your Father (Luke 6:37-38; 17:3-4; 1 Peter 3:8-9).

The last three "necessary qualities" are those that specifically apply to us as Christian parents.

*Faith.* When our children first enter perplexing adolescence and we seriously examine the world into which they're moving, we feel overwhelmed with apprehension. Inadequate to protect them ourselves, we turn to our almighty, all-knowing, ever-present God. And our prayers take on a new depth, a new urgency. Faith assumes a practical quality as never before, for we have little choice but to daily watch them walk away from us and to trust them to their heavenly Father (Ps. 27:1; 139:1-18; 144:12; Prov. 14:26).

*Prayer.* Make prime time for lifting your children before the Lord! Pray that God will guard and guide your teenagers, that He'll shape and mold them into the people *He* wants them to be. Pray for openness and understanding between you—that your bond may be comforting and indestructible. Joyce Landorf admonishes parents to pray for their children's best friends, as well, that they may be a good influence, not a harmful one. Pray for yourself, too, that God will equip you to be the wise, joyful mother of a teenager (Ps. 145:18-20; John 16:23-24; James 3:17-18).

*Dedication.* Your young people may seem resistant to the faith of their fathers (and mothers). Yes, you make it your goal to worship as a family and to see that your teenagers are involved in the life of their church. Regrettably, however, many young people temporarily rebel against their Christian faith, as well as other parental values.

Realize that you may be able to force your teen to go through the motions of church involvement, but you can't control the heart. You may, in fact, strengthen your child's resistance by your insistance. Nevertheless, don't let it affect your own commitment. If your teenager steadfastly refuses to attend worship service, you'll have to give in and give up eventually, but don't capitulate at the first protest. Don't be dogmatic or bitter, but don't be timid, either.

*Authenticity.* Avoid laying on a guilt trip when teens reject church attendance. Rather, be prepared to share, calmly and gently, what your faith means to you. Think through why you go to church and be prepared to let your children ask hard questions. They may remain unresponsive, but they'll respect you as one whose faith is real and alive—not, as is sometimes suspected, a mere going-through-the-motions. And your words, the sincerity they see on your face and hear in your voice, will linger in their memory. That may be just the wedge that will open the way for the Holy Spirit to reach them.

Encourage teenagers to express their questions and uncertainty about faith. (If Christianity can't stand up under close scrutiny, it's not worth much.) Urge them to be honest with God. A heartfelt statement such as, "God, if You mean what You say in the Bible, if Jesus is real, then let me know it!" is not blasphemy. Young people who ask such questions are searchers, seeking answers. Even the great people of God have had their periods of doubt. So do you and I. Can't we patiently bear with our children in love, even as our merciful Father accepts us?

In the meantime, let them see you living out your faith (Gal. 5:22-25; Col. 2:6-7). They'll be watching, even if they appear not to be—and with teens it's action that counts. For example, if you remind Christy of the Eighth Commandment when she repeats a rumor about a classmate, but you later run down the lady next door, what will stick in her consciousness? If you scold Brent because he can't get along with his younger brother, yet you're not speaking to Aunt Betty, which will make the deeper impression?

So let them see Christ in you. Then if there is a departure from active Christianity, it will likely be transitory (Ps. 103:17-18). Take comfort in knowing that your child may have moved away from God for awhile, but God has not reciprocated—He has his hand on your young person (Ps. 145:8-9). The faith principles you instilled are part of your son's or daughter's character, even if they seem to be dormant at the moment. God's Word is never without effect (Is. 55:11).

*Perspective.* If your teenagers are dissatisfied with your church, examine it from the viewpoint of a young person. How's the youth group? Are there *attractive* activities for teens? Is there spiritual food geared for their tastes? Are there meaningful opportunities to serve? Do your children have a reasonable number of peers within the congregation? Are the services and sermons applicable and appealing to young people, as well as to those middle-aged and older?

If you don't like the answers, what can you do about it? Talk to your pastor first. Volunteer your time. Study successful youth programs in other churches and interview the leaders to find transferable concepts. But don't just sit there—do something! You can't blame your children for disinterest if there seems to be little aimed specifically at their age group.

Some parents have gone so far as to transfer membership to another congregation, but that's a last option. And it's usually not even possible in smaller towns or rural areas. If you help raise the effectiveness level of your own church, it's best of all, because then many young people will benefit!

## *Strength for Your Journey*

You can see by now that mothering teenagers is a growing experience—for mother. Or, as some have put it: Parents don't raise children; children raise parents! If you're new to your task, you may feel uneasy. That's natural with any new challenge. But if you're a Christian mother, you need not fear. You are blessed! First of all, you have the Holy Spirit living within you, so you also have His gifts (Gal. 5:22). And you will need every one of them as you—and your children—progress through their

>wonderful,
>wacky,
>frustrating,
>exciting,
>trying,
>laughing,
>maddening,
>satisfying teenage years.

Think of the mountaineer who struggles, stumbling and falling at times, striving to reach the summit. At last, exhausted but triumphant, the climber plants both feet on the pinnacle of the craggy peak and surveys the marvelous view.

Compare that to the wonderful moment when your then-grownup child will say to you, "Mom, you're my best friend,"—and mean it. Then like the climber you'll declare, "It was all worth it! Every bump and bruise, every frustration and tear, every tortuous step of the journey . . . to reach this point, I'd do it all again!"

Keep that enticing prospect in your mind's eye and draw on it when the going gets rocky. Concentrate on it when you need a second wind.

And don't forget to enjoy the journey! Your child's turbulent teen years will be over before you know it!


**For Further Reading;**

Campbell, D. Ross, M.D. *How to Really Love Your Teenager,* Victor Books, 1981. Christian-oriented; good communication techniques; discusses how to understand, relate to, and express your love to teenagers.

Dobson, Dr. James, *Preparing for Adolescence.* Vision House, 1978. Christian-oriented; covers preteens and teenagers, with strong emphasis on building self-esteem.

Ginott, Dr. Haim G. *Between Parent & Teenager.* MacMillan, 1969. Communication techniques for parents and teens; good insights, but sometimes moves rather slowly.

Ridenour, Fritz. *What Teenagers Wish Their Parents Knew About Kids.* Word Books, 1982. Christian-oriented; lively, practical style by parent and counselor; focuses on three areas of concern: self-esteem, communication, and authority; tips on developing key attitudes.

# 5

# Nurturing and Nourishing in Special Situations

## The Single Mother, the Stepmother, the Adoptive Mother

*Love does not die easily.
It is a living thing.
It thrives in the face of all life's hazards,
save one—neglect.*
      James D. Bryden

*You can give without loving,
but you cannot love without giving.*
      Amy Carmichael

*A father to the fatherless, a defender of widows,
is God in His holy dwelling.
God sets the lonely in families . . . .*
      Ps. 68:5-6

*He settles the barren woman in her home
as a happy mother of children.*
      Ps. 113:9

Whether you're a mother raising your own children alone, one who acquired a ready-made family when she said "I do," or the mother of a child of your heart but not of your womb, you face some challenges peculiar to your status. The previously stated principles of strengthening the mother-child bond are applicable. But women who've slogged a few miles in your sandals will tell you that there *is* a difference!

## *Solo Mothering*

*I*f you're a single mother, you carry a wearisome load—and that's no news to you. In fact, it's easy to get bogged down in that. One of the sometimes overlooked blessings, however, is that you and your children will likely grow closer, perhaps because of your shared pain as well as your more exclusive relationship. Yes, your youngsters will need time to adjust to the divorce or to the death of your spouse. They'll go through a grief process of their own, even as you do. Their hurt, as yours, will be part of the healing.

But it's often difficult for children to understand, much less verbalize, what they're feeling. Some parents mistake the stiff-upper-lip facade for healthy adjustment. And since you, too, will be in the process of adjustment, you'll inevitably be self-absorbed. "I was so wrapped up in my own pain that I guess I just didn't realize how my kids were hurting," says Yvonne. "Oh, sure, I'd ask them, 'How's everything going?' and they'd answer, 'Oh, great, Mom. Everything's just great.' I'd be so relieved to hear them *say* that . . . Then I'd tell myself at least I didn't have to worry about them, too! So I'd breathe a big sigh of relief and take them at their word.

"Later on, of course, I had to deal with it. And my heart ached for them when I finally realized that they'd been bleeding inside for months, and I hadn't noticed. What I should have done right away was to sit down with Rachel and Todd and ask them whether they understood what was happening," Yvonne continues. "I kidded myself that kids get over things more quickly than adults, so that was why they didn't talk about it more. Yet they needed an opening to share their anger and fears—and so did I. Eventually we worked it through, but not without professional help. We all would have been spared a lot of loneliness and misery if I hadn't put off the inevitable."

Yvonne's experience is common. So it's good to set up a family conference early on. (If you're divorced and you haven't had a talk like this before, do it now. To use an old cliché, better late than never.) Draw out your children's feelings and encourage them to be completely open about their emotions. Reassure them that it's all right to express feelings of rage or resentment or rejection. Otherwise they may turn those emotions inward, where they'll fester and spread.

You've probably read that children often blame themselves, especially in the case of divorce. They remember the times that they disobeyed or disappointed the absent parent and conclude that that's the reason for the departure. So you'll want to talk it through and help them to realize that your marriage breakup had nothing to do with them.

Just as you confessed to God your own responsibility in the death of your marriage, be open with your children. Reiterate that the trouble between you and your spouse had *nothing* to do with them and admit that you, too, were part of the problem. (Be aware that even when one spouse feels that the other is totally at fault, counselors say that's almost never true.)

You'll want to be honest about the facts, both of what happened and of your present situation—depending on their age and comprehension, of course. But put the best construction on everything, especially their father. Reassure them of his continuing love, even if that appears unlikely. They need to hear that for their own security. If there are financial problems, such as nonpayment of child support, don't continually remind them that their father is a chump (even if he is).

Remember that children need to feel that their parents are good, loving people, no matter how much evidence there is against that. It's important to their concept of themselves. So being bitter won't benefit anyone, even you, in the long run. Neither will trying to reinforce the right on "your side" or to prove your innocence. If you struggle with such emotions, this would be a good time to pray together, asking God to help each of you to live in forgiveness and love, even though it may be awhile before the hurt is healed and the pain fades away.

Your children may be grappling with other secret worries. Children of divorce often fear that the remaining parent may be the next to leave. Then they will have been abandoned by both Mom and Dad. So it's good to broach that topic, even though they may never hint at it (because they're afraid you might reveal that their worst fear could be true). Assure them that your love for them has not changed, that *you* will never walk out on them no matter how tough it gets.

Remind them (and yourself) that you are a family, a *complete* (not "broken") family, because you have each other and lots of love. And you have God, your loving Father, as well, whose hand is on your family. He will guard you and guide you and eventually bring good out of your collective heartache. Somehow. Some way—even though at the moment that oft-quoted promise (Rom. 8:28) probably seems a cruel mockery.

Share your own feelings, too, and don't be afraid to cry. Your tears—and your children's tears—are healing, cleansing. It's the unexpressed sorrow that's destructive. Even if you, too, wanted the divorce, perhaps initiated it, you're bound to feel sadness. When a person—or a marriage—dies and is no more, there is grief. There is loss. There is emptiness. Before one can move on, one must face it, accept it.

## *Competing for Affection*

*I*f you're divorced, you may experience a common pattern: Your children go to visit Daddy; he takes them all the places you can't afford, showers them with gifts. Then they come home and tell you what a marvelous time they've had. Perhaps you feel that you can't handle one more gushing word about dear old Dad! Bear in mind, however, that if you turn cold or become sarcastic, you'll put a distance between you and your youngsters. Suddenly there will be something they can't talk to you about. Might that not hurt you more?

Should your ex-husband remarry, your children will be in a quandary. They'll wonder whether it's disloyal if they learn to like or love their new stepmother. How should they act? What do they call her? What do they tell you?

You may find yourself struggling with unexpected feelings yourself, wondering whether this will alter whatever peace and arrangement you've hammered out so far. You may envy his new happiness, feel a touch of jealousy, feel like a "have not" to his "have." And you'll be curious, tempted to have your youngsters spy out the situation and give you a blow-by-blow report each time they're together. That, of course, is unfair. You need to accept her; your replacement will have an influence on your children. Your positive attitude may help ensure that her influence will be pleasant and constructive.

Your best tactic—best for your children, best for you, best for your ex and his new wife—is to assure your offspring that it's okay to love their stepmother, because love has no limits. Tell them that it's good that Daddy won't be alone anymore. (And try to believe it!) If you need to get a message through or talk something over with your ex-husband, do it firsthand. Don't make your children your go-betweens, nor pawns in a battle to determine "whom they love most." For their sakes cooperate with your ex-husband and his wife, or your children will be the victims.

Difficult as it may be, try to understand that your children's father is probably hurting, too. Perhaps that's why he packs their visits with so many activities and presents. He feels guilty because he's absent during their day-to-day life. Logically, he knows that he can't make up for that with trips to the zoo and stuffed animals, with video games and front-row seats at the hockey game. But that's all he can think of to do.

Conversely, some fathers can only cope by staying away. Seeing their children causes them too much pain, reminds them how much they're missing. Most of the time such men block it out of their minds, but when they see their children, they realize what the divorce has cost them. And so they cut off contact.

Whatever your particular situation, resentment and recrimination will accomplish nothing positive. Peace will come when you give your own pain to the Lord and ask Him to take the burden—and keep it (Phil. 4:7; Col. 3:17). He has not forgotten you (Ps. 40:1-4; 56:3-4, 8). He alone can bestow healing and enable you to live in forgiveness (Rom. 15:5). Once you can give up your hurt, you can move on. And so can your children.

You should be aware of one readily available hazard. Single mothers sometimes fall into the trap of becoming too emotionally involved with their children, turning to them for support and nurturing that should come from other adults. (This is not meant to suggest any sort of sexual involvement.) Such mothers rely on their child to fill all the empty places in their lives. The youngster, sensing the mother's need and perhaps a bit flattered at being Mom's confidant—just like a grownup—fails to develop healthy relationships with peers.

Take Laura and her son, Brad, as an example. When Pete died, Laura told her son, "You're the man of the house now, son." Ten-year-old Brad squared his shoulders, smiled a wavering but reassuring smile at his mom, and walked tall. But small shoulders aren't meant to carry such a heavy load. In many ways Brad stepped into Pete's shoes. Laura brings home her problems from work and seeks Brad's opinion. They've settled into a comfortable pattern. Brad takes an active part in decision making. They share their leisure time, cook as a team, and really enjoy each other's company. Neither has friends from their respective age groups, but they don't care. They have each other, and that's enough.

Togetherness is wonderful, but every child and teenager needs to develop relationships with peers, or they can be emotionally incomplete. They need the freedom to act their own ages. Single mothers require some distancing, too, to keep their own perspective. Laura, for instance, unconsciously views and treats Brad almost as a miniature adult. Yet he *is* a 13-year-old boy.

Last year Brad wanted to go out for sports, but Laura wouldn't hear of it. "You might be injured—then what would I do? You're all I've got now!" At Laura's suggestion, Brad has taken up photography instead, and they've equipped a darkroom at home. Now the two of them often go on weekend field trips. Laura is delighted. "He's such a good kid—has never caused me a moment's trouble!" Laura tells her sister, Kate. Kate observes that Brad seems happy enough. Thinking of her own son, Joe, who's not the least interested in family activities at age 14, Kate feels a twinge of envy. Yet she senses intuitively that something's not quite right . . .

91

The missing piece is balance. Hanging on too tightly has interfered with growth, for both mother and child. Too much closeness (even between husband and wife) can cause us to become ingrown. Your mother-child relationship, already made more intense simply because there's no father in the home, is meant to be the nucleus from which both of you go out into the world. Both mother and child shore each other up, support each other in love, give to the relationship—and let each other go. That bond is to be the comforting base, not the be-all, end-all of living. Because if it is, one day the child will leave, and you'll be devastated. Or else the child *won't* leave, unable to function alone. Neither alternative is what you want.

Remember, too, that youngsters need role models of both sexes. You can't be both mother and father to your children, nor should you try. But you can seek out males who are willing to include your children on outings with their own offspring. Do you have relatives nearby, or are there men in your church who could occasionally be substitute fathers? Perhaps you could trade off individually or fellowship in groups with other single parents. Single fathers need female role models for their children, you know.

Boys, especially, need such male perspective. Sons of single mothers often complain, "Mom won't let me do *anything*! She's always worrying about me. For Pete's sake! What does she want me to be—a girl? You'd think I was a little kid just learning to walk and she needed to follow me around to keep me from falling!"

Mother love, you say. Not really. That's "smother love." Children need room to grow. They need the chance to stumble and fall now and then so that they can learn to pick themselves up. It's natural to be a bit more cautious when the buck stops with you alone. It's normal to expect more of your children when you don't have another adult in the home. And it's wonderful to have a close mother-child relationship.

The point is that you walk a fine line between healthy companionship and unintentional interference with your child's emotional development. Not because you're "sick," but because you may be lonely and in pain. So now and then do a self-evaluation. Just don't suppose that your children can fully meet your emotional needs, nor you theirs. You're blessed to have each other, . . . but each of you needs space apart from your very precious togetherness.

## Mothering His Children

Stepmother. That's an unfortunate term, isn't it? For too many years it has been connected with poor Cinderella. But thinking people know that when you marry a man who already has children, you acquire a lot of challenges along with your new family. If you weren't a special kind of woman, you wouldn't even consider it!

So how do you go about bonding with these ready-made kids? Begin with a subtle change of mindset. Strike from your speech the phrase "his children." Think of them as "our children." And when you introduce them to your friends, say, "This is our daughter, Becky," not, "This is Burt's daughter, Becky." Just as you accepted your husband as he is, accept your new children as they are. You may observe (or even be the recipient of) behavior that's less than thrilling, but don't judge them or comment on their upbringing. Instead, be as loving and positive as you possibly can—and then some.

You may well face financial strain in your marriage because of your husband's child support payments or other financial obligations related to his "first" family. Jenny, for example, is forced to work because Marty's support payments don't leave them enough money to live on. "Every time I looked at Cass and Jessie I was reminded that because of them I can't stay home with *our* baby," says Jenny. "Yet their mother is home full-time and plays tennis three times a week! I'm glad Marty's the kind of man who lives up to his obligation, but I still struggle with my feelings. Yes, I knew the score going into this marriage, . . . but now I *really* know the score! I finally realized the fault doesn't lie with the girls, so at least I don't resent them anymore. That's progress."

If you're a weekend parent, his children will be in the way at times. That's inevitable. You'll sometimes be irritated to "lose" your husband to his children during what should be free time for the two of you. You'll feel left out when they remember old times. You'll want to be included—but sometimes they'll need to be alone. Let it be. Remember that it's important to your husband, whom you love, to spend time with his children. So make it important and acceptable to you, too.

## All Day, Every Day . . .

*T*he full-time "second mother" sometimes envisions sweeping changes in the stepchildren's behavior, their eating/sleeping patterns, study habits, and the like. But don't try to revamp their lifestyle all at once. Go slow. They have enough to cope with, just getting used to you. And vice versa.

Allow plenty of time, too, to feel comfortable with each other. At first you may watch every word. They may not know what to call you. "Mom" would seem disloyal. So talk about that and decide together. The children may withdraw or be sullen or angry or hard to handle. (Or you may luck out, and they'll just be themselves.) Whatever your particular situation, one day they'll do or say something that pushes you to your limit. You'll stop being diplomatic; you'll yell a bit, as every other mother does occasionally. Perhaps the children will respond with their own honest feelings—perhaps calmly, perhaps screaming at you, perhaps crying. Some families "happen" without that confrontation, but many do not. So don't feel frustration and guilt if you have a blowup. Feel joy! You're on the way to being real with each other.

"When Ted's boys came to live with us, I walked on eggs," says Susanna, "and so did they. We were so polite to each other that it was sickening! They'd disobey, and I'd pretend not to notice. They'd fight, and I wouldn't say a word. I knew they were testing me, but I was determined to stay calm and in control.

"One day they went too far, and I just blew my top! I started shouting at them in the same way as I do with my own daughter sometimes. When I realized what I was doing, I was so ashamed . . . Then I noticed that Matt and Sandy were screaming right back at me—yelling that they wanted their mom and dad to be back together, that they didn't even like me and stuff like that. I started to cry, and they stopped and looked so scared.

"But then I began to laugh," Susanna continues. "For the first time we were risking ourselves with each other. We had taken off our masks, and it felt good! I was so happy I just held out my arms to them, and they came, and I hugged them close. That was the beginning and from then on, things started to work out. Now at our house, what you see is what you get!"

As much as possible, cooperate and coordinate with the children's biological mother. Be a peacemaker—for their sake as well as for your husband's and your own. With weekend visits, try to strike a balance. Include some chores and everyday activities. Maybe what they want most is just to sit on the couch with their dad (and you?) and watch TV. Although you're not a Monday-Friday family, try for things that make memories. Celebrate birthdays on the closest day you're together. Bake a second birthday cake or freeze some homemade ice cream. It doesn't matter what you do, just so it's special.

Check out read-aloud books from your public library and take turns reading. Let the children help you cook. Teach them a new craft or fun songs. Have toys and playthings and games available and try to "their" own bedroom(s). When your new children walk in the door, you want them to feel they're coming home, not coming to visit.

Decide what your house rules will be and communicate them to the youngsters. It seldom matters whether your dos and don'ts are the same as at their "regular house." Children soon learn which behavior is acceptable in each.

## *Open Your Heart*

*I*t's difficult, maybe impossible, to bond with people you don't know. So step one in forging your relationship is learning to be open and vulnerable. "After the explosion, the boys and I sat on the floor and really talked—for the first time," says Susanna. "I told them that I didn't know much about mothering boys and that I wasn't sure I could do it. I told them how much I loved their dad and that because they were his sons, I loved them before I ever laid eyes on them. I told them that if we worked together we could be a real family, but that even if they didn't help me out, I wasn't going to give up. I said there wasn't anything they could do that would make me stop loving them. Funny thing is that for the first time I really meant it!

"Before I'd been too fearful to ask them how they felt about coming to live with us, but now I figured it was time to let it all hang out. At first they wouldn't say much. But then they started talking, and all the hurt and anger and fear poured out. They cried and I cried and we hugged and kissed each other. Tom had taken my Cindy to a concert, and when they got home, we talked some more. Finally we were beginning to be an honest-to-goodness family. Wouldn't say that was the last time the boys made me angry," Susanna continues, smiling. "Sometimes they still threaten to go back to their mom when they're mad. But I know they don't mean it, and so do they. It's no bed of roses, this stepmother business. But I really love those boys, and I'm glad they're living with us!"

Years ago mothers used to caution their young adult children, "Take a good look at his (her) family, because you're not only marrying one person. You're marrying all of them!" Today's stepmothers would echo, "And how!"

Sometimes your task may seem an impossible challenge, but you're not alone. Your gracious God is with you, so call on Him for strength, for understanding and patience (Is. 40:27-31). Most of all, trust Him to be your Source of love (1 John 4:12, 16).

### *Mothering the Chosen Child*

*P*erhaps you've known the anguish of being unable to conceive. You've been through the endless tests, followed the procedures, charted your body's cycles endlessly. Maybe the doctors found a reason, maybe not. Whatever the cause, you do not have the longed-for infant with your eyes and your husband's dimples. Only pain that never quite leaves. And so you decide to adopt.

Or you may have simply decided to adopt a child. You've opted to raise someone else's child rather than—or along with—your own. Perhaps you're rearing one or more foster children.

Whichever you are, there are a few relationship-strengtheners unique to your situation. First, try to find out as much about your child's biological background as possible. That will be much easier to accomplish in the beginning than it will be later on. Include any details you've observed, as well as the official data, but omit any facts or opinions that could be hurtful for your child to discover later. Gather as much information as you can and organize it while the facts are fresh in your mind. Write it down in detail—don't trust to memory. Put it all in a packet and store in a safe place, such as a safe deposit box.

Like many adoptive parents you may feel, "Don't bother me with the details. Just give me my child!" Later, however, you may wish you had a ready reference. And should your child predictably raise questions about birth parents later on, you'll be prepared. The evidence you provide will testify to your loving thoughtfulness. That can keep such curiosity from becoming a wedge between you.

If you adopt an older child, you may be able to visit back and forth beforehand. Then you'll have the start of a relationship even before the child moves in with you. If you can, take photographs of your child's home, teacher(s), and friends. (Get the names, too. It's up to you whether you'll make them available to the older child now or simply store them in the file.) Anything you can find out about your child—favorite subjects and activities in school, food preferences, etc., can also aid you in helping your child to adjust. If possible, bring along some items from your child's former bedroom: a pillow, stuffed toys, a picture from the wall, or some favorite books.

Some adoptive parents want to make contact with their child's biological parents if it's legal in their state. Others try to ensure that there's no contact at any time. Opinions vary as to what's advisable. The question is, what are *you* comfortable with?

"I was so glad that I had a chance to meet with the young girl who gave birth to our Nicholas," says Janine. "We liked each other at once, and I was reassured when I realized that Amy was healthy and bright and emotionally balanced. She had to be! She had carried Nicky to term, and although the prospect of giving him up made her desolate, she knew he'd be better off with us than being raised by a 15-year-old.

"Amy saw that Ryan and I have a solid marriage, too, and how much we wanted a child. We asked a lot of questions, wrote down answers, addresses of grandparents, and so forth. We took photos of Amy, too. When we parted, we made a mutual pledge. She promised that she'd never interfere, and we promised to send her pictures of Nicky every year on his birthday. I want our son to know how much his natural mother loved him and how hard it was for her to let him go," Janine continues. "I think it will make Nicky feel more secure to realize that he has *two* mothers who love him dearly!"

"Not me!" says Carolyn. "I'll tell Jessica that she's adopted, of course. But the thought that her birth mother might one day show up on our doorstep terrifies me! In fact, we moved out of the area after the adoption. I don't know that woman, and she doesn't know me—and I hope we can keep it that way."

No matter what the laws and practices are in your own state, one thing is sure: the climate is changing, and more adopted children then ever before seek to learn about their biological parents, whether or not they actually make contact. Sometimes this becomes a life-or-death situation, as in the case of a genetic weakness or disease that may arise. (Such individuals may need to know about their family medical history in order for doctors to prescribe treatment.) Your goal, then, is to bond so strongly and securely with your chosen child that such a meeting could not erode your loving relationship for either of you. That's a far more positive way to proceed than simply seeking to prevent such contact and thus live in fear.

## Turn "I'm Adopted" into a Plus

*B*egin by becoming comfortable with the word *adopted* yourself. Use it in natural conversation while your child is an infant (or from the beginning, if it's an older child). Don't wait until the time is "right," to announce that fact. Have books available that talk about adoption and read them aloud. That's a subtle way to make the concept ordinary and routine. Make your family history a personal tale and emphasize how you desired the child.

"Nicky's favorite bedtime story is the one about him," says Janine. "He's been hearing it since he was a baby, but he never gets tired of it. It starts with how much Mommy and Daddy wanted a baby to love, but we just didn't have one. So we searched and we searched and we asked God to give us just the baby that He wanted us to have. We asked God to have His angels watch over our baby, even though we didn't know him yet. Then one day the telephone rang, and a voice on the other end said, 'Can you come and get the beautiful baby boy we have just for you?' And, oh, Daddy and I were so happy that we jumped up and down for joy, and we hugged each other and we told everybody we knew that our baby boy was here!

"Then we met Nicky's first mother, and she was such a nice lady—and pretty, too. She told us how much she loved Nicky and how sad she was to give him up. The only reason she was able to do it was because she didn't have a happy home where Nicky could grow up with a mommy and a daddy," Janine continues. "That's what she wanted for her baby boy. And when we held Nicky in our arms, Daddy and I were so happy that we thought we'd just burst! We kissed him and hugged him and just loved him to pieces! Then we brought him home to our house and laid him in his very own crib in his very own room in his very own house. And the three of us have been happy, happy, happy ever since because Nicky is our *adopted* son, and that means he's special.

"We always end the story the same," says Janine. "Every night when Daddy and I say our prayers, we thank God for Nicky. And we thank Him because out of all the little boys and girls in the whole wide world God picked out Nicky just for us, because He knew that we are supposed to be a family!"

"Michael and I made a family album for Leah," says Carolyn. "We had a friend take a picture of us looking sad because we didn't have a baby to love. We took one of the nursery, the baby crib, and the high chair, all empty, of course. Michael took a photo of me in our big rocking chair, waiting for a baby to rock to sleep.

"The day we went to pick her up we took lots of pictures, both there and when we got home. Now Leah was in the crib, and I was holding her in the big rocking chair. As she grew and developed, we added more photos. We put them in one of those albums with the clear plastic over the top. We started 'reading' it to her when she was about a year old. Before long she could carry 'Leah's book' all by herself. She'd bring it to us, and we'd go through it and tell her all about it and how happy we are to have her. She loves that book!"

With a few adaptations the same idea would work with an older child or a foster child. After all, wouldn't every child love to hear that they're special, that they're loved, that their parents are thankful to have them? A story and such a photo album also build a sense of family identification, and that's vital with *any* youngster, but especially with one who's adopted.

## *Be Patient*

Some adoptive parents and children make an easy adjustment and seem to meld into a family quickly. For others the process can be lengthy and, sometimes, very trying for everyone—but especially the parents. They dreamed of a sunny-natured, laughing youngster who would fill their lives with love. Perhaps they got, instead, an angry child or an apathetic child or one who's sad. Some children run to you with open arms and a spirit of rejoicing. Others sport emotional armor against being loved—they're too afraid that they'll be hurt again.

With an older child the transition will be easier if you're able to let the child get acquainted with you and your surroundings beforehand. Still, bonding may take longer than you expect, even if you do everything right. You'll be offering what seems to you new-and-improved-plus-lots-of-love. But your child may stubbornly cling to old-and-familiar-is-better-no-matter-what. Try to understand that familiarity, even if it was a bad situation, often spells security. Don't be too hard on yourself, either, if your child is nonresponsive. Hang in there and don't set deadlines. Day by day you're building the foundation that will enable the child to trust and love you. The relationship *is* taking root, whether you can see the evidence or not. We're all human beings, not machines which can produce instant emotion when we press a button.

So let your youngster set the pace. For example, it may be awhile before the child is ready to wear the new clothes you so happily bought. You may prepare pizza with all the trimmings or other special treats only to have the child ask, "Can I have a peanut butter sandwich?" Don't try to make your child over. Time enough for a different hairstyle and new shoes and good manners later. Too many changes feel like pressure. Besides, right now this youngster is coping with a new home, new parents, perhaps a new school, and almost certainly a new neighborhood, if not a new city. That's quite enough!

Realize that any change, even a change for the better, involves loss. Your child is coming *to* you but also coming *from* somewhere else. So there will be grief. If your youngster exhibits denial, contrariness, irritability, bargaining, or withdrawal, consider these normal stages of what's come to be known as the grief process. Eventually acceptance will come and the child will be ready to move on. So encourage your new son or daughter to be up front about feelings—and don't you place a value judgment on which are good and which are not.

## *Love That Doesn't Quit*

You are the adult, presumably the mature, balanced person in this equation. So whatever your child dishes out, give back love and acceptance, with as much calm as you can muster. Let your child discover by experience that your love is durable, not dependent on his or her attitude.

> *Love is patient, love is kind. It does not envy, it does not boast, it is not proud. It is not rude, it is not self-seeking, it is not easily angered, it keeps no record of wrongs. Love does not delight in evil but rejoices with the truth. It always protects, always trusts, always hopes, always perseveres. Love never fails . . . .*
> *And now these three remain: faith, hope and love. But the greatest of these is love (1 Cor. 13:4-8, 13).*

That's the kind of love that every mother needs, but especially those who adopt an older child. And it will likely be a first in that child's life to receive love like that. So wait out the rough weather. Just, as they say, go with the flow and allow plenty of time for that sense of family to grow. You can't *make* it happen, although many of the guidelines outlined earlier in this chapter will be helpful. But you can communicate your love through action, by being accepting and supportive. Try, too, to use the term *our family* frequently; plan family outings; make decisions as a family, etc. The child most unlikely to seem enthusiastic often needs shared family activity the most.

To help reinforce the sense of unity, Evelyn Felker suggests that "restructured families" decide on their values and then try to live them out in practical ways. For example, your family might decide that it's important to help people with needs, to reach out to the lonely, and to learn to know people from other backgrounds. To put that into action, you might work together to pack a grocery box for the needy, invite widowed Mrs. Smith for Thanksgiving dinner, paint Grandma Johnson's fence together, or host an exchange student. Choose any project that translates theory into deed and can be carried out together.

As an adoptive mother, you especially want to work on reinforcing the child's self-esteem—and you may literally have to start from nothing. Older children up for adoption have often been in and out of several foster homes. One rejection after another. Such children judge that something must be wrong with them, otherwise someone would want them, someone would care. If your newly adopted child doesn't respond as you'd envisioned, it may be because of deep fear that this can't last, that another abandonment is inevitable. Shutting you out is the child's logical defense against future pain.

Take the pain *you* feel at this temporary rejection to the Lord and ask Him to give you a supply of love that will endure. Remember that everything worthwhile takes time. Once you've been tested and found trustworthy, your child will almost certainly respond. Your steadfast love will be the rich soil in which the seedling of your two-way mother-child relationship will burgeon and bloom.

## For Further Reading:

Felker, Evelyn. *Raising Other People's Kids*. Eerdmans, 1981. Christian-oriented; complete guide for relating to foster children, adopted children, and stepchildren.

Peppler, Alice Stolper. *Single Again—This Time with Children*. Augsburg, 1982. Christian-oriented; for the parent made single by death or divorce; examines emotions of children, discipline, sharing responsibility.

Reed, Bobbie. *I Didn't Plan to Be a Single Parent.* Concordia, 1981. Christian-oriented; advice for the single parent, including how to resolve legal issues and develop a supportive network.

──────────── *Stepfamilies—Living in Christian Harmony.* Concordia, 1980. "Stepfamilies can be successful if each member recognizes that the relationships are fragile and need to be handled with prayer."

# 6

# Strengthening the Ties That Bind US— While Cutting Them
## The Young Adult

There are only two lasting bequests
we can hope to give our children.
One of these is roots;
the other, wings.
    Hodding Carter

Him that I love, I wish to be free—
even from me.
    Anne Morrow Lindberg

When I was a boy of 14, my father was so
ignorant I could hardly stand to have the old
man around. But when I got to be 21, I was
astonished at how much he had learned
in seven years.
    Mark Twain

When your young adult child moves out of the family home—whether it's to a college dorm, an apartment, or to share a home with a brand-new spouse—there's a touch of finality about it. Even if he or she will be home on weekends and holidays, somehow you both sense that this is a milestone event. One chapter ends and another begins. Yesterday you held the infant on your lap. Today the young woman or man is ready to function without your input or help.

If not accomplished before, this is liberation time—for your child and for you. After all, isn't that what you've worked for all through these growing-up years? Of course! Yet it's seldom as clear-cut as it sounds. We've all howled at the patter of comedians, the cliché of comic strips, and the stereotypical clutching parents of movies and television. We laugh because these characterizations contain sometimes disquieting glimpses of truth. People who inhabit such situations, however, rarely find them funny.

Twenty-six-year old Mark made his big announcement at the obligatory Nelson family Sunday dinner. "Hey, everybody, I have big news! I've had an offer for the job I always dreamed of, and I've decided to take it. Penny and I will be moving to Denver next month. Isn't that exciting?"

His mother looked stricken. "Why, how can you even consider going way across the country?" she asked in a hurt voice. "After all those years Dad and I waited for you to finish school! Now that you finally have your degree you want to just pick up and leave? We were looking forward to having life a little easier once you came into the business, what with your father's heart and all . . . But it's *your* decision, of course . . . We wouldn't dream of interfering in your future."

Later Mark said, "I walked into that house on cloud nine and slunk out carrying a king-sized guilt trip. All afternoon Mom was dabbing at her eyes, and Dad was staring out the window. I expected some flak, but I don't know if I can handle this . . . Maybe I do owe them more after all they've done for me. And what if something happened to one of them? I guess I'd hold myself responsible. I feel like I won't be happy if I stay, but now I can't feel good about going, either."

Sometimes parents who manipulate via guilt are those who always held extremely tight reins. When their teenage children seemed increasingly less impressed with their parents' opinions, as is the case with most young people, they hung on to control by issuing ultimatums: "As long as you live under this roof, you'll do what I say!" When their young adult child finally gets "out from under," these parents lose their leverage and must find a new method to retain a measure of influence. Some such parents are afraid of being alone and see this as a way to ensure at least "duty" communication. Whatever their motives, those who employ guilt may be open or indirect about it.

But no matter how cagey and subtle parents think they are, their children read the real message they send—and they resent it. Andrea is a successful, single career woman, age 23. "Someday I may marry, but right now I like my lifestyle as it is—if only my folks would lay off! My mom keeps sending me clippings from the hometown paper about weddings of my schoolmates and their new babies. And Dad asks whether I've 'found Mr. Right.' I do love them, but the more they pry, the more I clam up and withdraw. It's my life, and I'll get married if I want, when I want, to whom I want!"

Many young marrieds feel heavy parental pressure to produce at least one grandchild. Heather and Kevin have been happily married for five years. Each has a good job, and they're buying their first home. To an outside observer they appear to be every parent's dream children. "But my folks won't be happy until we have a baby," says Kevin. "You'd think we don't count for anything without kids. They tell us that of course *we* have to decide, but in a thousand other ways they're saying the opposite."

## Cut the Cord!

Some parents, whether or not they're aware of it, try to buy a chunk of control. When Kim wanted to move into her own apartment, her divorced mother seemed very supportive. "But she's never really let me go," muses Kim. "Mom calls at least once a day and comes over several times a week. She always brings something for the apartment or some goodies or maybe a blouse she picked up for me at a sale. I appreciate it, but I want to be my own person and make my own way, even if I have to live in a shack and eat peanut butter! Mom drives me crazy, but she's given her life to raising me, and I wouldn't hurt her for anything. So how can I walk away? I'm all she's got."

Unfortunately, these examples are not rare. Dr. James Dobson, well-known Christian psychologist and author, recently conducted his own mail-in survey. Of the 2,600 replies he received, 89 percent of the respondents felt that their overall relationships with their parents were strained. Almost half (44 percent) said their parents had never really let them go nor accepted them as adults.

Part of the problem is simply that for many parents, their offspring—no matter what their age—will always be "children." And that can be comical—at least to the rest of us. For example, there's the mother who scolds her 40-year-old daughter, a respected professional, "Annie! Don't you know better than to keep your house key on the same ring with your car keys?" Another mother cautions her son, age 55, "Don't forget your rubbers, Charlie; it looks like rain." A father chides his 22-year-old son, "Isn't it about time you got a haircut?"

Yet the fact is that we reach a point when our parenting role largely becomes obsolete. Knowing that intellectually, however, doesn't always translate into practice. In fact, it usually requires a conscious (sometimes lengthy) process of rethinking. Looking back into our own life, comparing what we thought about ourselves at a similar age, is often helpful.

"When our daughter planned to move to a large city a couple hundred miles away, I was panicky at the thought of her being on her own!" confides Nancy. "Had a whole list of reasons why it was a bad idea. After all, she seemed so young! One day I realized that when *I* was 21, I'd had two babies, a husband out of work, and a mother-in-law who lived nearby and was dying of cancer. No one hinted that I was too young to cope with all that, so I just did! I remember feeling very proud, very mature, at how well I was handling it. So I guess I owe my kids the same gift my parents gave me early on. I'm giving them the freedom to make their own decisions and then to pay the price."

Letting go is seldom easy. After all, for many years our function as responsible parents has been to direct and comfort, to counsel and to care for, to love and to provide for our children. They've been our joy—and our frustration. The cooking, cleaning, and paying the bills we can give up with a hurrah. But every human hungers to feel necessary and needed, so it's a natural to want to hang on to that nurturing facet of parenting. Let's face it: our children don't need it—*we* do!

Yet the separation must come, one way or another. Many counselors note that at some time in their development young people *must* put distance between themselves and their parents, must psychologically sever those connections that bind, if they're to become capable, self-ruling adults. If that rebellion didn't surface during adolescence or teen years, we may see it now. Depending on the individual's temperament, it can be a mere ripple or a raging storm.

If the break involves open hostility, there will be pain all around. Comfort yourself with the knowledge that for this particular person, at this stage in life, it may be a necessary step to adulthood. If handled wisely (accepted with equanimity and continued love, rather than as a personal attack), such revolt is almost always a temporary phase. Once young people have "proved themselves" to their personal satisfaction, they'll likely return emotionally, anxious to establish a new relationship.

Be aware, too, that even if they leave home feeling friendly, they may get around to writing or calling only infrequently. Your best approach is to stay in touch yourself. Write friendly letters which tell about funny happenings in your family or the neighborhood. Share your feelings on what's happening in the world. Clip cartoons and comic strips you think they'd enjoy. Send newspaper and magazine articles that pique your interest and ask how that struck them. Don't pry into their personal life or lay on guilt because they haven't answered your last six letters. Just write regularly—whether they answer or not—and call now and then. Build a bridge so they can come back when they're ready.

## Foundation for Friendship

*T*his is a time when we learn to disengage from the old parent-child relationship ourselves so that we can replace it with another, just as satisfying and enduring: friend to friend. One essential for friendship is respect for each other. This differs from that implied in respect-your-parents-and-elders. Rather it's accepting our offspring *as they are,* without reminding, rebuking, or trying to remake them. Since our main effort during our children's growing-up years has been shaping and molding them, however, it's admittedly difficult to put away what has become a habit.

Yet that's exactly what's required if we want their freely given love rather than grudging filial obligation. Remember, too, that when we seek to retain control or to manipulate our children, they can't be comfortable around us. After all, think how we avoid those who one way or another convey, "You don't quite measure up."

Few of us would consider telling our adult friends how to live their lives. That's a good way to lose a friend! Still we make no apology for telling our grown children what we think of their choice of companions, their lifestyles, their purchases, etc. "It's for your own good," we say. But our suggestions and "constructive criticisms" become walls, not bridges. The more we seek to clutch and control, the more we lose. Eventually we're left with an empty shell of a relationship, muttering to ourselves, "I don't understand it. I was only trying to help that ungrateful kid!"

Respect for our children also means that we count them capable of solving their own problems, so we avoid unsolicited advice or assistance. If they call to discuss a problem, we don't jump in with an immediate solution or opinion. Rather, we assume that they simply want to talk it over with someone they trust. As we would with one of our peers, we listen without interrupting and encourage our child to explore all aspects of the situation. And then (ideally) we say, "I know you'll make the decision that's best for you." Because whether we like it or not, since they must live with the results of their choices, it has to be up to them.

Another aspect of respect sometimes involves taking the initiative to end any parent-child connection that could hold them back. As an example, subsidizing a college education can go on too long. Audrey and Phil are wondering about that very thing. "It seems that Jay has been a student forever!" she declares. "He started out with one major, got his degree, then decided to change his emphasis. Now he's working on his master's, and I suppose he'll want a doctorate after that. We've been paying his college costs and some of his living expenses so that he could do well in school. Lately it seems that he only calls when he needs money.

"We love our son," Audrey asserts, "but how long are we expected to support this big baby? Yet, if we stop now, he may throw in the towel, and all those years will just be down the drain."

Parents who long past the norm financially support their child (or who assume responsibility in another way) need to ask themselves some hard questions:

Do I pay the bills because I'm committed to my child's aims?

Do I see my checks as proof that I'm still needed?

Do I feel that I have nothing to bring to this relationship—no guarantee that Mary will stay in touch—unless she's dependent on me?

Is my financial support a way of keeping control?

There are no clear-cut answers as to when to cut off support. Parents must evaluate each situation individually and decide for themselves. But sometimes the most beneficial thing we can do for our children is to say, "Enough!" Thereafter they may waver, they may stumble, they may go through some rough times. Still, isn't that exactly when you and I began to grow up and become responsible? And didn't we feel good about ourselves as we learned to cope?

## "I Want to Do It My Way!"

Another parental task is to determine who owns which dreams and goals. Once we've clarified that, it can be easier to accept diverging points-of-view. For it's hardly necessary to note that the life choices of our young people may differ from our own goals for them.

Parents who believe strongly in higher education, for instance, are often dismayed when their child decides to skip college. Curt's parents had scrimped and saved so that he could have what they'd lacked—a college education. Curt chose, instead, to be a mechanic. "Nothing I like better'n working on cars! So why should I work like a dog for four years and end up doing something that couldn't possibly be as much fun?" he asks. "Besides, I've seen too many pals with diplomas who can't find work in their fields. My folks can't see it, but these days that sheepskin doesn't guarantee a thing!"

Such differences have ancient precedent. Parents always think they know best—and so do children. Freedom for both comes with remembering that our children are *not* extensions of us. Rather they are (or should be) independent individuals, free to seek their own way, free to stumble, even free to fail—and to learn from each experience.

A major difficulty for most parents, especially Christian parents, lies in accepting the more casual sexual behavior of so many of today's young people. It goes against our personal values and certainly runs counter to Scriptural admonitions against fornication. Those of us who thought we were raising our children "right," i.e., in a Christian home, are dismayed when a daughter or son begins living with a lover, for instance. We know all the dangers, both physical and emotional, and we fear for the aftermath. Increasing numbers of young people, however, see nothing immoral about it.

"It broke my heart when my Maria moved in with Tom," says Ramona. "I asked my daughter how she could do such a thing when she knew it was wrong. Over and over I begged her to break it off, but she wouldn't listen. One day she said, 'Mamma, I am staying with Tom. I don't want to hear another word about it! If you don't stop this, I will leave this house this minute, and I'll never be back!' One thing I know about my Maria; when she gets that look in her eye, she means it! So what were we to do?

"My Carlos, he said we have to drop it, that's all, or we could lose our daughter, maybe for good. So now she comes home for family dinners, and we all try to make her and Tom feel comfortable. We don't like it, and we'll never think it's right—but we keep our mouths shut!" Ramona continues, with a rueful smile. "What else can we do?"

If your grown children never disappoint you, you'll probably make history! That, too, is part of parenting. In some situations we'll probably feel conscience bound to confront our son or daughter. As Christian parents we'll want to point out what the Bible says about their life choices. Our best approach is to talk with our child openly, quietly, lovingly. But it's crucial to emphasize the forgiveness and strength available to God's children, rather than to dwell on guilt and punishment. And we'll concentrate most on our own feelings and misgivings, not on trying to prove our child wrong.

But having stated Scriptural principles and our own emotions—and especially our love!—it's best to let it drop unless our child brings it up later. Harping on his or her foolishness or wrong choices may cause our beloved child to walk out of our life. Then we lose all chance to be a godly influence, to offer counsel, or to be a support if (when) our child is in pain or need. We're to take our example from our heavenly Father, who forgives and accepts us unconditionally, all through our lives.

You may be saying, "But I feel so disappointed!" So was the father of the rebellious, ungrateful, and estranged prodigal son. But he welcomed his penitent son home without a word of reproach. Can we do less than to demonstrate our unchanging love and our emotional support?

And how many parents have anguished over a child's choice of marriage partners? We're older and (supposedly) wiser; we spot character traits that telegraph future difficulties. We look at our child, caught up in the euphoria of love, and wonder whether anything we say would sink in. The answer is, "Probably not." Most parents find that when they speak against their child's love interest, the son or daughter immediately becomes defensive and more determined than ever. Should it come down to choosing between parents and the beloved, the parents will almost certainly lose.

"When Suzanne told us she wanted to marry Aaron, I wanted to blow up!" Martha exclaims. "He was so totally wrong for her! Aaron comes from a totally different background, another religion. He's much older than Suzanne and has three children from his two marriages. Mel and I saw him as a rotten risk for marriage and a grab bag of endless problems. We talked and we pleaded, but Suzanne stood her ground. One day she simply announced, 'I *am* going to marry Aaron, with or without your blessing. What happens next is up to you.' Then she walked out the door without another word."

Tears glisten in Martha's eyes as she says, "The next few days were awful. Finally I did what I should have done in the beginning.

I asked the Lord to melt my dislike of Aaron and my fears for Suzanne and to help me accept Aaron. I even asked God to give me love for Aaron, though I couldn't imagine that! More than anything I didn't want to lose my daughter, and I just gave her to the Lord all over again.

"The Lord didn't just zap me into being crazy about Aaron. But after Mel and I talked it over, we called them and then met them for coffee. We told them that if they loved each other, we'd welcome Aaron into the family. And we pledged our support and our love. Hardest thing I've ever done!

"They've been married three years now, and they seem happy," continues Martha. "The problems we anticipated are all there, but we bite our tongues rather than say, 'I told you so.' Mel and I would like our daughter's life to be as smooth as silk, but we have to admit that Aaron has been a good husband to her. And a real miracle happened somewhere along the line—I've learned to truly love Aaron!"

## Your Love-Gift: Freedom to Be

*I*t may be worth mentioning that we parents and in-laws need to allow our adult children the same courtesy and privacy we accord our friends. So we always knock, even if we have a key. We rejoice that they have their own friends and activities and wouldn't expect them to change their plans on short notice. We offer our opinion only when asked—and then with the same consideration and tact we exercise with other adults. We feel no claim on our children's holiday or vacation time.

It helps us to make this transition if we can recognize that these young people, single or married, are no longer part of "our" nuclear family. (That doesn't imply that they're cut off from the family or excluded, simply that we don't matter-of-factly expect them to join in as before.) Rather, each is a new "family unit." As such they'll be making plans and setting goals of their own—and they should.

Suppose there's too much separation. Suppose days, weeks, even months go by when you haven't see your child. The phone doesn't ring; the mailbox is empty. Call and say hello if you like, but conquer the urge to impart guilt! Otherwise you may, indeed, receive duty phone calls, letters, or visits, but probably little more. Better to assume that your adult children are healthy, happy, and managing well. Then when you do hear from them, you'll have the satisfaction of knowing it's because they want to be in touch.

In every situation, in fact, the wisest strategy is to "put the best construction on everything," as Luther admonished in his explanation to the Eighth Commandment. Our paramount aim is to keep communication alive between our children and ourselves, for if we lose that, we may never regain it. That often requires that we simply swallow our objections and opinions. In short, it means that we cut the proverbial cord and let them go, armed with the certain knowledge that we'll always be there if they need us.

Isn't there something else we can do? Yes. We can pray. Our children are in God's hands, now as always. Pray for guidance for your grown children, just as you prayed during their growing-up years. Pray for their welfare—emotional, physical, and spiritual. Pray for the strength of their marriages and their families. Pray for their protection and for their health. Our active parenting days may be over, but our praying days go on forever!

We need to remember, too, that what our children need most as they leave our homes and establish their own lives is confidence. For in spite of their excitement and their seeming nonchalance, anxiety frequently lurks beneath. After all, they're doing everything for the first time, and that's always scary. They hunger to know that they're accepted and have our unqualified love, no matter what.

In fact, it's vital to continue to demonstrate your love—in all circumstances. Don't let your hugging and touching be part of your child's past. Often these young adults yearn to be held and reassured—and need that even more than when they were children. They can't admit their fears and misgivings now as they did when they were three. (After all, haven't they often been told, "You're too big to cry?") Probably they'll fiercely maintain their cool, calm exterior and lock their fears inside. Don't question them. Just open your arms to them, speak your love, affirm them.

One last point—but it's major. During those inevitable clashes or times when you disapprove of your children's actions, never be afraid that expressing your love implies approval. They probably knew all along how you felt. At any rate once you've voiced your reaction and conveyed God's truth to them, there will be no doubt.

Your love, your friendly, nonjudgmental attitude, says only one thing: you love your child unconditionally. You hate the sin, but you *love* the sinner. Now you're allowing your young person the freedom to make choices—even wrong choices. To put it another way, you're saying to your child, "I recognize that you've grown up. You're now an adult, responsible for your own life."

At this stage of our children's lives we help them most by being supportive, demonstrating by word and deed that we *know* they have what it takes to make a success of their lives. There's only one way to do that—to let them go, with no strings of guilt or control or obligation attached. Only when they feel truly free will they come back of their own accord, ready to participate in our new relationship as loving friends.

## *Attitude Checklist*

**W**hen I think of relating to my child as to a much-loved friend—an equal—I feel . . .

I show my respect for my adult child by . . .

How have I deliberately shown my child that I accept him (her) as he (she) is?

I can see my adult child growing when I observe . . .

These are some qualities I like about my child (name at least three):

These are some qualities I like in my child's spouse:

Some ways in which I can enhance the relationship with my adult child are . . .

Are there changes God would have me make in this relationship? (Rom. 15: 1-2, 7; Eph. 4:1-3; Col. 3:12-17; 1 John 4:7-12).

# 7

# They Keep Coming Back Like a Song

## The Drop-in, Drop-out Adult Child

*Home is the place where,
when you have to go there,
they have to take you in.*
   Robert Frost

*Children need love, especially
when they do not deserve it.*
   Harold S. Hulbert

*There is no love which does not become help.*
   Paul Tillich

*There is nothing so loyal as love.*
   Alice Cary

*Love seeks one thing only: the good of the
one loved. It leaves all the
other secondary effects to take care of
themselves.*
   Thomas Merton

The children are through school and out on their own. No more orthodontia, college tuition, extra car insurance premiums. Peace. Freedom. Joy! Alone at last. At this stage of our lives we can look forward to travel and leisure and putting ourselves first for a change. Right?

Not necessarily.

Somebody changed the signals in the middle of the game. Look around you. How many of your contemporaries have grown children living at home? You may be surprised as you tally it up because many parents would answer, "Oh, we usually have one or two at any given time. They come and they go."

They come to pay off school loans or to accumulate the rent deposit on an apartment. They come because they were in an auto accident, and now they're paying off the loan on the wreckage and also making car payments on a replacement, so there's little money left over to live. They come to think through which, if any, college major they should finally choose. They come because living costs are sky-high and they're not earning enough to maintain themselves in the style that is "rightfully" theirs. Besides, Mom and Dad aren't perfect, but at least they're a known quantity, which is more than you can say about a roommate you obtain via want ads. They come because it has become respectable—even fashionable!—for adults to live with their parents. Some of the adult children leave again. Others recognize a good deal when they get it.

The drop-in, drop-out generation. Victims, they think, of a world built of sifting sand, where some idiot might blow you up at any moment. Refugees from an uncaring society, they return to their first place of safety: home. They've had a look at the big wide world of adulthood and gainful employment and found it wasn't nearly so thrilling as they expected. Like Peter Pan, they don't want to grow up.

The extended family, several generations living together in one house, is a commonplace lifestyle in many parts of the world. In America, too, there was a time not so long ago when couples often lived with their parents until they saved the down payment on a home of their own. One or more unmarried relatives might move in and help with household chores in exchange for room and board.

Or elderly parents no longer able to maintain their own home would live with one of their married children.

In more recent times the goal of every young person was to be out from under Mom and Dad's watchful eye. The mark of maturity was to be on one's own, no longer dependent (and thus beholden) to anyone. Now the pendulum is swinging back. It's no longer a touch disgraceful to be 28 years old and unemployed, living with one's parents, with no immediate expectations of change. In fact, it seems to be a national trend. Parents may chafe at the arrangement, but feel perplexed. Should they kick their own flesh-and-blood out on the streets?

Some adult children return for a specific reason. They have a goal, and both parents and child understand that this is a temporary situation. These young people are secure within themselves, but they need a bit of help for awhile in order to achieve their purpose. They know who they are and have worked through their concept of independence. They're comfortable returning to the parental home and can relate on an adult-to-adult basis with their parents. For the most part these are the parents and children who can function as supportive friends, each contributing to the relationship.

There's another group of homecomers, however, whose motives are less defined. Some have grown up with a certain standard of living which they've come to regard as their due. They've bought the pervading myth that money and things guarantee happiness, that purchasing bestows pride. Since they're not able to live where they want, to wear the expensive clothes they crave, or to dictate their lifestyle by choice instead of economics, they don't want to play the game anymore.

Some of these adults are simply immature, spoiled brats. Others feel inadequate to cope with what's expected of them as an adult. They don't run forward to life, exhilarated at the challenge: they retreat and withdraw. They're willing to exchange a large measure of their self-worth and independence for relief from the responsibility of taking care of themselves. It's the people in this second grouping who can become longstanding problems. No longer children, they're not ready (or willing) to become adults.

Sometimes their parents are a contributing factor and give tacit approval by sending out the hidden message that it's okay not to grow up. They have themselves adopted the notion that each person is entitled to "the American dream" and so pity their offspring who, they feel, are missing out. These parents provide so much TLC that they *encourage* their children to be leaners all their lives. Perhaps they look back and yearn for the child-rearing years. Nothing else has proven quite as engrossing. No other worthwhile activity has given that same satisfaction. They need to be needed. So when their grown children return to the family home they can almost kid themselves that they're reestablished in their earlier more important position. That may feel good for awhile; it's nice to be needed! But in the long term it's not a healthy way to relate, for either of them.

So guard against making it too easy, too comfortable, for your drop-in adult child. If you meet every need—give everything, demand little or nothing—you remove any incentive for this young person to return to a world that often feels cold and lonely. And the longer your daughter or son stays, the more difficult it will be to gather up courage to try coping independently.

## *Caught In-between*

You may find yourself caught in the middle between your parents and your children. The former, locked in a losing battle to retain their own independence, may require more of your time and attention and concern than ever before.

On the other side are your adult children—daughters or sons or both who are, you judge, way past the age to settle down, but who haven't yet "found themselves." Most are not neurotic nor manipulative. They don't intend to stay forever (although it can drag on a very long time). They are sufferers in the anguish of unhappy love affairs; would-be renters who can't quite swing it; perennial students who were told that education is the key, yet can't locate a job in their fields; the weary unemployed, sporting fragmented egos; the walking wounded from the divorce battlefield, some with children of their own.

They are your offspring, whom you love. They come to you for restoration, for time to get themselves together, for financial assistance—for a haven.

So how are parents to respond? We expected this period of life to be a time when we could congratulate ourselves on a job well done and begin to indulge ourselves. Reality may be quite different. What does love require? How do we truly help our children? Most of all, how do we preserve and reinforce our mother-child relationship?

"It does get sticky sometimes," says Katherine, "even though Bill and I get along well with our children. Over the past few years they've all been here at one time or another, even though our youngest officially departed five years ago! After trial and error we've got it down to a science. First thing we do is to make them really feel welcome. After all, it's not easy to admit that you can't quite hack it! We give them lots of love, too—hugs, kisses, talking. We don't ask a lot of questions, just give them time to get their bearings.

"After a day or two they usually get around to telling us what's going on. If they don't, we ask if they'd share whatever they're comfortable with. And then we listen *without* interrupting—no matter how many times they stop and start, no matter how long it takes. We don't try to tell them what to do—they're over 21!" continues Katharine. "And since they own the problem, not us, they have to decide what to do about it. Friends of ours, who learned the hard way, gave us two unbreakable rules: (1) Never pry. Grown kids have a right to privacy and parents do not have the right to know every detail. (2) If it's a marriage problem, *never* take sides! Don't enthusiastically agree if your daughter, for instance, says that your son-in-law is a rotten loser—even if you think he is. Later she may regret having revealed so much. And if the couple makes up, she could feel that you won't understand why they reconciled. So then there's a barrier between you."

## Who Pays the Bills?

*E*arly on you'll also want to discuss practical details. Who will do what? It's good for everyone to be responsible for their own belongings and their sleeping quarters. Usually it works out best if everyone participates in kitchen chores and periodic cleaning, too. Or you might want to set up a schedule and change off. If your adult child has an income, part of it should go toward costs of goods and household expenses, unless you've agreed to forego this so that your child can accumulate a reserve fund.

How long does your child plan to stay? Take the individual situation into account. A person recovering from a divorce will need more time, presumably, than one who's between apartments. Don't leave it open-ended, or you may find yourself two months down the line, wondering how to bring it up. You can always renegotiate later, if it seems advisable.

Should there be small children involved, the picture becomes a bit more murky. Who will handle their care? Are you willing to babysit your grandchildren? Anytime? How often? Remember that the care of your grandchildren really is their *parents'* responsibility, so don't feel guilty if you're not able or inclined to babysit full-time.

Feel free to set the standards within your own home. For example, if you don't want your adult child to bring home an overnight guest of the opposite sex, this is the time to spell it out. If you expect to be called when your child will be late, say so now. Even if you're uncomfortable, it's easier to work this through matter-of-factly in the beginning and to set up target dates. Otherwise antagonism may build up, and it could become a touchy subject. At this point you're examining possibilities; later on the same discussion may feel like placing blame.

## *You Can Help with the Healing*

**P**erhaps your adult child is simply sorting things out. Perhaps all that's needed is time and peace and the security of feeling loved, with no strings attached. So supply that. Or your grown-up child may be hurting. If so, you're feeling the pain, too. But bear in mind that you can no longer take on the role of dragon slayer. By the time individuals reach adulthood they need to realize that their problems are their own. Others can empathize, even advise. But no one else can discern the solution, nor implement it.

So as you interact, try to view the circumstances through your child's eyes. As always, do more listening and loving than talking.

Be a sounding board, not the resident authority. Avoid pronouncing judgment—on persons or ideas. Relate in love, walking alongside, being supportive, but separate caring from carrying. You cannot bear your child's burden any longer. And if you want this young person to become a fully functioning mature adult, you shouldn't even try! See yourself and your home as a temporary splint for the brokenness—which will heal, not as a permanent artificial limb, meant to make up for what's missing.

Whatever the reason for the upheaval, your young person's self-esteem may be just about destroyed. Your task is to help in the rebuilding process, but you can't accomplish that by speeches, no matter how flowery. "It was a real struggle to convince Andrea of her self-worth," says Carmel. "She was in the midst of a divorce from Brian, and both had been tearing each other to shreds. I tried giving her pep talks, but of course, that didn't make a dent. For a long time she was too shattered to land a job.

"Finally I decided that she probably had the same needs as when she was a child. So I hugged her and touched her often. I began quietly affirming her whenever I could. Kept my eyes open for things she did well, for times she looked especially pretty, for situations I thought she'd handled well. She'd contradict me, but I didn't quit. Later, when she'd talk about her day at work, if I could pick up on something and compliment her, I did. And if I caught her putting herself down, I'd point out how she was distorting the facts—being too hard on herself.

"Slowly it began to sink in, but it was an uphill battle! She was just devastated. She'd dated Brian for so long and was so sure they'd have the perfect marriage . . . Then it went sour—or they gave up on it—in just a couple of years. Andy felt that if she could be wrong about something she'd thought about so long and hard, then she must be stupid or insensitive or just an incredibly bad judge of character. It took awhile, but I think she's come around the corner now. She's about ready to fly on her own again," says Carmel. "It's been a rough year for her, but I look at my Andrea now and see a woman who has a strength and maturity and depth of character that wasn't there before. I'm glad I was here—and I'm thankful that God could salvage something out of that wreckage!"

In your conversations with your grown children, do share the counsel of God's Word. But do so in a thoughtful, loving way. Be open about situations in your own life when you needed God's strength to get you through. Instead of preaching what your child should do, point out the lessons *you* learned and let the young adult figure out the personal application. As the saying goes, "God has no grandchildren." Each person at some point must make his or her own faith decisions. We can illustrate (and agonize), but our children themselves must decide what they'll believe. They're accountable for themselves.

The one thing *we can* know for sure is that God is faithful: "The steadfast love of the Lord is from everlasting to everlasting upon those who fear Him, and His righteousness to children's children . . ." (Ps. 103:17 RSV).

# 8

# *Keeping a Good Thing Going— for Life!*

*A child is someone who passes through your life and then disappears into an adult.*
    Unknown

*The past always looks better than it was. It's only pleasant because it isn't here.*
    Finley Peter Dunne

*I am not afraid of tomorrow, for I have seen yesterday, and I love today.*
    William Allen White


"The past is past," they say . . . but not for mothers. Our children may be adults and gone from our homes, but they're always in our hearts. A photo, a song, a chance remark, and we momentarily glimpse again . . . the rosy-cheeked baby in the crib. . . little hands "finger painting" with oatmeal . . . the toddler's unsteady first steps and gleeful pride . . . pint-sized Sunday schoolers piping, "Jesus loves me, 'dis' I know, for 'duh' Bible tells me so" . . . children giggling under the covers at naptime . . . kids running through the yard, capturing lightning bugs in a peanut butter jar . . . sturdy bare feet delightedly stomping through summer puddles . . . glowing faces around the dinner table, happily slurping spaghetti . . . young piano players, groaning as they practice . . . the tremulous angel in the Christmas pageant . . . long, athletic legs carrying strong young bodies around the ball diamond . . . the determined 12-year-old covered with suds, attempting to shampoo a 4-H calf . . . the quivering lip of the youngster waiting for a broken bone to be set . . . teenagers whose "life is ruined!" because of a new pimple . . . slumber parties with 4 a.m. pizza . . . corsages and formals and tuxedos . . . dejected young drivers (but alive!) and crumpled family cars . . . beautiful brides and nervous grooms, embarking on a life together . . .

Memory, the great makeup artist, smooths out the wrinkles, fills in the rough spots, and highlights the best features on the face of years gone by. With our selective vision we see only the good. And, of course, now that we have 20/20 hindsight, we can also see the richness that was hidden in the pain. There was a purpose and, whether we recognized it or not at the time, there were good years.

So it's easy to get stuck in the past, to feel that the best is behind us. We sigh, sure that if we could only go back and do it over, *this time* we'd have more understanding, more patience, more . . . *This time* we'd wouldn't make all those dumb mistakes raising our children! (Instead, we'd make new ones.)

But it really *is* the irretrievable past. We can't change one minute or one day of what's behind us. All we have is the present. If we live it wisely, today and tomorrow will be good, too—for ourselves and for our children. It's really not so difficult. We need a bit of a love 'em and leave 'em alone attitude.

First, last, and forevermore, let your child be his or her own person, living his or her own life. Give up for all time any claim to telling your grown children how they should do things or to pointing out their mistakes. They have the right, just as we did, to make wrong decisions, to act foolishly. The consequences of such actions, too, are theirs—and theirs only. The time is past when we need to feel ashamed or embarassed by our children. They're old enough to stand alone.

## Pointers for Parents

So how do we relate to our adult children? With respect, as to a much-loved friend. We set them free emotionally to live their lives—and we go on with our own. We're supportive, publicly and privately. We're kind and considerate, and we speak well of them. True, we have all the old "parent tapes" in our heads, but we don't have to play them. It's mostly a matter of choice—*our* choice.

Do you want your children to write and visit and telephone you because it's their duty? Or rather because they enjoy you? If the latter is our desire, we'd better clean up our act! For if we nag them, criticize them, ridicule their choices, why would they want to be around us? Would you desire company like that?

Should they be so wrapped up in their own lives that they "forget" you, choose to rejoice! Busy people are usually happy people. Besides, if you must manipulate them by laying on guilt, any gestures of affection toward you will be empty of meaning.

How about you? Can you handle it if your children decide to go skiing over Christmas vacation, even though it's "your turn" to get them? If they overlook your birthday, will you sulk? Will you sigh and cry? Will you "unintentionally" manage to convey that you feel hurt and lonely?

Keep up your end of the relationship, nevertheless. When letters don't arrive and the telephone doesn't ring, don't get bogged down in self-pity. You do your part. Write anyway. Give a call now and then—no guilt attached! You maintain the bridges today, and tomorrow your relationship will still be alive, so your children will cross over those bridges to you.

Be their unflagging cheering section! Cheerleaders don't call the plays; they don't analyze; they don't bark orders. They don't quit cheering just because someone makes a blunder. They're ready with encouragement at every turn, even if sometimes they're not quite convinced that they're rooting for the best team. They keep on cheering their team to win, no matter what the odds.

Keep your opinions to yourself. *If* they ask (and if you can be diplomatic), feel free to offer your thoughts. Otherwise be Mrs. Positive. Does this strike you as insincere, hypocritical? Think it through. If what your children decide is important to them, you do want it to work out, don't you? And should they be wrong, will your saying so help them in any way?

Affirm your support. There's a crowd of people ready to crow, "I told you it would never work! I knew you were wrong from the beginning! Any fool could have seen that that was a mistake!" So instead of you, too, pointing an accusing finger, tell them what you've learned: the only people who fail are the ones who never try.

"Adopt" your in-law children. If (when) your child chooses a marriage partner, *you* choose that person, too. Accept your new family member unconditionally. If you have fears, doubts, or criticism, speak them (only) to the Lord. Let *Him* design and carry out any necessary alterations—that's not your responsibility. And ask the Holy Spirit to flood your heart with love for this person your child loves.

(In the early stages of a romance, of course, you can offer your counsel. If you observe qualities that seriously trouble you, do voice them lovingly. But once the couple becomes serious or decides to marry, your negative comments will become a wedge between you and your child.)

Untie the apron strings. When a couple exchanges marriage vows, they become "a family." Your child's primary loyalty and obligation rightfully belongs to his or her spouse (and children). Parents and siblings are to assume a less important status. That's God's plan (Gen. 2:24).

In all things, concentrate on the good and the positive. Never allow yourself to be a divisive element or force your child to take sides. Watch your tongue, too. A mother or mother-in-law's fault-finding and negative attitude can be the "acid rain" that slowly, almost imperceptibly, erodes the young marriage. So be a booster!

Recognize that becoming parents is a personal decision. Do you want grandchildren? Most of us do. But that's a commitment that each couple must accept or reject by themselves. You judge life incomplete without children—they may not. And since raising a family is an 18-year assignment, minimum—no vacations, no overtime, no weekends—it's only fair that they alone should determine whether they want to take on the job.

## *The Anguish of Divorce*

Support marriage. Do all you can to foster and shore up your child's marriage. Even Christian couples experience divorce, true, and it seems to be a growing trend. Your place as a parent is to be loving and nonjudgmental, while at the same time offering the timeless truth of God's Word, which addresses the topic in clear language (Mal. 2:14-16; Matt. 5:32; 19:3-9).

Those words are uncompromising. God's standard for marriage is the union of a man and a woman—body, soul, and spirit—into one flesh (Gen. 2:23-25). And it's to be an indissoluble union. God allowed divorce as a temporary concession, out of mercy. In that day a woman could be discarded at her husband's whim—no provision for her security, no property settlement. But God's precept was—and is—that marriage is for life.

Today we as a society are wrapped up in our own wants and needs. We've lost the desire or willingness to go the extra mile (Matt. 5:41), to forgive without keeping count (Matt. 18:21-22; Luke 17:3-4), to put aside our own concerns for the welfare of another person or for a principle (Rom. 12:10; 15:1-2; Phil. 2:3). These are not fashionable concepts! Today divorce often occurs because one or both marriage partners have reached the point where they feel, "I've had it! I don't have to put up with this any longer!"

Unfortunately, concentrating on another's faults can make us blind to our own. So those who "escape" often find themselves in another marriage where the stage props and the leading man have changed, but the plot proves remarkably similar.

Know the Scriptural guidelines and think through your own feelings on marriage and living. Share them lovingly with the troubled couple, but don't preach. Encourage them to seek counseling, either from their pastor or from a counselor he recommends. Keep an open mind yourself and avoid being drawn into the problem or taking sides. Your goal is to aid the preservation of this union, but you're not in control, nor is it your responsibility.

In the end, of course, it's another of those up-to-them propositions. So one day you may be watching your beloved child endure the painful procedure of divorce. Your heart will ache, too, for you know perhaps better than your child just what's being abandoned. Assure your child that your love is undiminished—that his or her image hasn't tarnished in your eyes. This individual has enough hurt already.

Besides, you do love these young people as much as ever. You're just sad for them and disappointed that what seemed so full of promise could wither and die and be discarded. Don't be too judgmental.

Making a marriage work is never simple, but at least in earlier years the pressure was to stay married. Consequently more of us rode out the inevitable storms—and gained the strength and confidence in each other that comes from surviving together, knowing each has proven reliable. Today's young couples face ever-present propaganda of *self*-fulfillment at all costs, so their task is even harder.

God in His grace forgives all sin as we bring it to Him, including the sin of divorce. (The hurt and the grieving process will still be very real, however.) Our loving heavenly Father may choose, too, to bring great good out of the scrap heap of your child's broken marriage. Your part is to be an agent of healing, to simply trust God, and to leave the future in His hands.

## *Put the Good Stuff In!*

*B*e an affirmer, not a reformer. Have you told your children *now* what you would say of them were they to be suddenly killed? If not, this is the time. Never say or do anything which feels unloving or disloyal. Be a source of strength, spiritually and emotionally. Reinforce their strengths—they likely know their weaknesses at least as well as you.

Take the positive approach. Make your letters and phone calls witnesses to your faith and hope and good outlook, not recitals of problems and despair. You want your children to feel better about themselves, their lives, and their future after an interchange with you. As when they were children, they look to you, the "voice of experience," as their role model. Expect the good, and you're far more likely to get it.

Keep the communication going between you. If that means swallowing negative comments, so be it. You may prove your point, but you could set up a climate that will be a hindrance to any real communication between you. You want a heart-to-heart relationship, not meaningless going-through-the-motions. Don't you?

Forgive yourself. The choices your children make may sometimes contradict your own faith and the principles you'd worked so hard to instill. If so, you'll likely feel pain—and probably guilt, reproaching yourself with an endless succession of "if onlys." Of course, you're wiser now! But you were as effective as you knew how to be . . . at that time, in those situations.

Our children have free will. That means, unfortunately, that they're free to mess up their lives. And they are responsible, as is every other adult, for their own behavior. As the jargon goes, "Remember who owns the problems" that may result from their unwise or inappropriate choices; don't adopt the difficulty as your own. (Incidentally, it's not up to parents to subsidize a lifestyle of which they disapprove.)

"Tough love" requires that adult children be allowed that greatest of growth experiences—living with the consequences. And that's hardest of all for us as parents. Yet we do them no favors when we rush in and bail them out. The prodigal son was welcomed back with genuine love and great joy, but his father never rescued him from feeding and dining with the pigs (Luke 15:11-32). The young man, after running with the wrong crowd and blowing his dad's money, finally came to his senses, repented, and returned—when *he* was ready. It's lamentably true for most human beings: the only lessons that stick are the ones we learn on our own (and usually the hard way!).

Pray for the Lord's timing if you feel you must confront your children about their lifestyle or actions. Don't just rush in and blurt it out. Ask the Holy Spirit to prepare the way for you and to give you the words. Remember that you're not there to judge or to advise but to share with them what you've observed—and what you've learned in your own life. What they do about it is, again, their decision. Now let the discussion—and your expression of concern or disapproval—rest.

In all things *you* be tenderhearted. Hate the sin but shower the sinner with your love. (Don't fear that this will be construed as approval—they know the difference. And the fact that you've not withdrawn your love may supply the extra strength that's needed to make the very changes for which you pray.)

Speak love. Put it into words! Write it in your letters! Demonstrate it with your warmth and your hugs! Give out nonjudgmental, no-strings love, and you'll get it back—full to the brim, pressed down, running over. Do it now, even if it seems awkward to you. There's no sadness like the regrets which haunt those who lose a loved one and remember all the things they never said. None of us have a guarantee how long we—or they—will live, so don't wait for the perfect moment.

Keep filling your adult child's bucket of self-esteem as you did in earlier years. It's a tough world out there. Be sure that your children feel they're okay in your eyes and loved *as they are*. Tragically, many people go through life thinking they're not quite as acceptable to their parents as a brother or sister who is (a) more talented, (b) better looking, or (c) more successful. Thus in their own point of view they never quite measure up, no matter how successful they may become in the opinion of others. What a waste!

Consider sending your children a note on Mother's Day, telling them of the joy in your heart because you're their mother. On birthdays don't just sign your name to a card; write a sentence or two about why you love this person. Sometimes reminisce about memories of their birth or childhood.

Keep their interests in mind. You may see a cartoon or a new item that you know they'd enjoy. Clip and send it to them in your next letter. They'll be delighted to know that they're in your thoughts.

## But They're Grownups!

**Y**es, they *are* adults. Grownups are supposed to be capable and self-sufficient—and they may have families of their own. But where is it written that any human being ever reaches a point where they don't enjoy expressions of unqualified love? For example, if you rise to the top—in any field—you'll have people who will "love" you because of what you've accomplished and probably because you're in a position to do something for them. But how wonderful to know that somewhere there's one who'll love you *just the same* if you one day find yourself on the bottom! Our children, at any age, hunger to hear us express that, verbally and written in black-and-white.

You won't always be here to do that, nor may your children. So do it now. Do it often! Cast the bread of your love on the waters, and it will come back buttered.

Be open and honest with your grown children. Now they're viewing you from an adult perspective. If you thought that you fooled them before, know that the older they get the less likely you can maintain the facade. Genuine love requires two honest, open, transparent people, so drop your guard. Admit your inadequacies and failures. (They see them anyhow.) If you can admit yours, they'll be free to share their own. That's when love can flow freely. That's when the bond grows stronger than ever, because it's between two real people.

## Be a Special Grandma!

Grow a good relationship with your grandchildren. Your children won't applaud you if it takes them three days to get their children back to normal after they've been with you. Leave the heavy-duty correction to the children's parents, but do uphold the family rules. Help your grandchildren to feel good about themselves by having time for them. (By the way, don't interfere with—or criticize—your children's parenting, unless you're convinced that their practices could have truly harmful effects on the children. Though you dote on your grandchildren, the fact is, these are *their* children.)

Make it your task to communicate unqualified love and to build your grandchild's self-esteem. Even if you're far away, you can nurture the relationship. See that your children have a photo of you. Give them one in a frame so that it doesn't end up in a box waiting to be mounted in an album. (That's not being critical, just realistic; most people are months—or years—behind. If you want your grandchildren to remember your face, such a photograph needs to be out where they see it!) You might give your grandchildren a snapshot of you to keep. If it's for a young child, mount it on sturdy cardboard and cover it with plastic.

Don't think you must always come bearing gifts, especially those that are costly. (Ask your children what the youngsters need beforehand. It's difficult for parents to rejoice over another frilly dress that's only worn on Sundays when their child really needs a couple pair of corduroys and some T-shirts.) Instead of a mass of Christmas and birthday presents, why not spread them out throughout the year? It's a very long time between those two days when you're a child.

Write to your grandchildren, too. Consider printing instead of cursive writing; children are more used to that and can pick out some words at an early age. The U. S. postage stamp is still one of the best buys around—and what child isn't thrilled to get mail of his or her own? You could record cassette tapes, too. For example, you might read a bedtime story or a Christian book for children aloud; then send the book and the tape so that the children can follow along. Or how about recording some anecdotes from their parent's own childhood—perhaps at a similar age?

Encourage your grandchild to mail you drawings and school papers so that you can display them on *your* refrigerator or bulletin board. (Perhaps your children could write their letters to you on the backs of these pages.) If you provide some lined writing paper and stamped envelopes bearing your address, you're more likely to receive a letter now and then.

Send each grandchild a package containing an inexpensive gift at various times throughout the year. Save freebies from cereal packages. Other possibilities are assorted stickers (kids love them!); balloons; fancy shoestrings; pretty hair barrettes; pencils imprinted with the child's name; art materials—colored construction paper, crayons, larger tablets of newsprint; and children's pages you've clipped from your daily newspaper.

Try to arrange one-on-one time with each grandchild. Go for a leisurely walk. Have an ice cream cone. Go to the park. As the children grow older, perhaps they could visit you for a few days or a week so that you can really get to know each other.

You may have biological grandchildren and those that are either adopted or stepgrandchildren. For the sake of your child, as well as the youngsters, do not differentiate between the two. Don't be like the grandmother of four who was passing around snapshots and said of the children of her two sons: "These two are the *real* granchildren."

Even though you never put it into words around your children, that labeling denotes the feeling in your heart, which will inevitably seep out around the edges. Such a response can emotionally damage the youngsters and it *will* deeply wound your own children. If they've been unable to conceive, they've already had their share of anguish. If they've adopted an older child or acquired a ready-made family through marriage, they face a sufficient challenge already. Don't add to it. So choose the attitude that says, "These are my grandchildren, beloved by their parents—and I love each one equally!"

How are you relating to your own parents? Whatever your answer, be aware that right now you're setting the tone for how your children will one day treat *you*. What they see in your attitude will almost surely be reflected in their attitude toward you. Good or bad, loving or unloving, critical or understanding, patient or impatient, helpful or disinterested, affirming or faultfinding—you decide. But recognize that you're setting yourself up for the same. A word to the wise . . .

## Don't Quit Now!

**B**ecome an intercessor. Continue to lift your children and their families before the Lord in prayer. Often they'll be too pressured, too mired down in the morass of daily responsibilities even to think clearly. You, however, know by experience that God is faithful, that He cares about every detail. So you can pray for your children with utter confidence, knowing that He knows exactly what lies ahead and what they need to meet each situation. Name your children and grandchildren individually in your prayers. Commit them to God's care and guidance and protection. Then sleep soundly at night, knowing that they don't walk alone. Entrust your own needs to Him, too, because He cares for you.

Stay mentally fit. Exercise your mind as well as your body, for the saying, Use it or lose it, applies to both. Read books that challenge you. Unlock the door of your mind and invite in some new ideas. (A closed mind usually telegraphs either ignorance or someone who's "set in her ways"—and you don't want to be either.) Keep up with what goes on in the world, with trends in our culture and in our nation, not just in your immediate circle of acquaintances.

Sign up for a class or workshop in something you haven't tackled before. Cultivate the friendship of younger people besides your own offspring. Being in a different stage of life, their comments and opinions will prove thought-provoking and keep you from being stuck in the rut of rigid thinking. Community college classes usually offer a stimulating mix of age groups, all the way from the late teens into the 70s and 80s—and you'll be learning, besides!

Keep moving. You needn't jog or do aerobics. Almost everyone can walk, and it's often termed the best exercise of all because it's far less stressful to one's body. Invest in a good pair of sneakers and form the habit of walking at about the same time every day. Prepare to be pleasantly surprised. You'll sleep better. You'll be more calm. You'll likely lose weight (or inches) because your metabolism will speed up. Unless you're already very fit, you'll notice improved muscle tone, plus more energy and endurance. Before long simple exertion won't leave you breathless. You'll also sport a more flexible body and more spring to your step. In short, you'll feel better, you'll look better, and you'll move better—even from just a half-hour's walk per day. And your health will improve in the bargain.

Keep up with the times. Are you still wearing the same hairstyle and makeup you adopted 20 or 30 years ago? Are the frames of your glasses in keeping with current styles? Do you choose clothing mostly because it's practical? Do you do and say and think in certain ways just because you "always have" and you're comfortable with it?
This is not to say that you should dress and talk and act like a teenager! The goal is to be an attractive woman, dressed and behaving in a manner appropriate to your age. Study the fashion pages now and then. Seek advice from a friend who dresses with a flair—or a helpful salesperson. Make the most of your appearance. Now more than ever, age is a state of mind. Yes, we are getting older. But we don't have to become "old"—and we all know the difference.

Cultivate your relationship with your Lord. Drink deeply from the well of His Word, in private study and through adult Bible classes. Ponder the meaning for *your* life. Store up God's truth in your heart so that you have something solid to give to others—especially your children. Aim to be a living example of the faith you profess, an authentic Christian. Since your time may be more flexible now, participate in retreats and workshops available through your church and church-related organizations.

## Where Can You Serve?

Consider, too, taking a leadership role in your local congregation. Every church needs people to lead Bible studies, teach Sunday school and vacation Bible school, sing in the choir, serve on the altar guild, make banners, help out in the office, and so forth. Perhaps you've always felt that "someone" should initiate a particular class or ministry in your church. Why not you? You've likely been growing in the Lord for many years, perhaps a lifetime. Like the apostle Paul, you *know* that in times of weakness we can draw on God's strength and depend on Him to carry us through. So you have much to share! You can speak, teach, or counsel with authority that God is worthy of trust.

Remember those earlier years when it seemed your life consisted of endlessly changing diapers and doing laundry and wiping noses and picking up toys and finding yet another way to fix hamburger? Remember feeling inadequate and outwitted as you parented a balky adolescent? Remember how you yearned for someone who would put a comforting arm around your shoulders and say, "I've walked my quota of miles in your shoes, and I want to tell you that you *will* survive! Let me share what I learned along the way . . ."

You could be such a mentor to a frazzled younger mother, either through your church or on a one-on-one basis (Titus 2:3-4). You don't need a college degree or special training. Your life experience itself, coupled with your Christian faith, qualifies you.

Try it out. Choose a mother who's younger in age or in years of mothering. Find someone with whom you feel at ease and just be a supportive friend. You may find it such a joy and so natural for you that you develop a real outreach, either informally or on an organized basis.

Regrettably, many woman who've reached this stage of life say, "I'm tired! I've done my share. Now it's someone else's turn to take over. I want to do my own thing for a change!"

But God has given us these years for a reason. He has filled our cups over and over again. He's been shaping and molding us so that He can use us. Think of yourself as a stream bed, fed by a spring of lifegiving water. Review your personal history. What have the past years equipped you for? How could you share what God has been teaching you and so enrich the lives of others? How could your insight and practical wisdom help someone else to cope more capably? Pledge your willingness to God; ask Him to direct your steps—and get ready for exhilarating adventure!

Though it may seem obscure, there really is a connection between the foregoing and strengthening your mother-child bond. To begin with, as you feel better about yourself, you're less likely to feel alone and abandoned now that those Very Important People—your children—have moved on to lives of their own. So instead of self-pity, you'll exhibit optimism and good cheer. Since you'll be more fun to be around, you'll likely see more of your offspring and maintain a deeper, much more satisfying, relationship.

Best of all, as you keep on growing spiritually, mentally, and physically, you'll remain productive. As the psalmist puts it: "The godly shall flourish like palm trees . . . . Even in old age they will still produce fruit and be vital and green" (Ps. 92:12, 14 LB).

The past is past . . . but a fulfilling life stretches ahead. What more could any of us ask?

# *Epilog*

Being a mother is a challenge—and a privilege—every day. As we carefully, thoughtfully nurture the living relationship with our children, as we water it with unconditional love, it will bear lasting fruit. For if it's true that a mother is the "most significant" person in shaping the child for life (and all research bears that out), is it not true that we're shaping the mothers and fathers of the next generation, who will shape the following generation, and so on?

The foundation of the bond between our children and ourselves is the love that Jesus Christ demonstrated when He laid down His life for us, His friends (John 15:12-17). As Christian mothers we, too, often lay aside our own hopes and dreams and desires for *our* friends—our children. That's not because we're inherently noble or self-sacrificing. It's because we recognize that love is more than an emotion; it's an action. And as mothers we have plenty of on-the-job opportunities to learn how to translate theory into practice. The often-quoted "love chapter," 1 Cor. 13, gives us a standard against which to measure.

All of us, now possessing 20/20 hindsight, see our own past deficiencies. We can't go back, of course. But we can go forward!

Begin by confessing your sin and shortcomings to your merciful heavenly Father and leaving the tiresome load with Him. Then accept His forgiveness and forgive yourself. If your children are older, you may want to ask them in a loving way for their forgiveness, too, especially if you feel that there are lingering effects from your inadequacies and blunders. Trust the God of reconciliation to heal past hurts and to bring good out of the debris of your failures. Trust him to melt the barriers and to establish love that keeps growing. There's no abyss so broad that love cannot leap it. No mistake so irrevocable that love cannot wash it away. No act so terrible that love cannot forgive it.

Realize, however, that the birth of restoration comes only after you annihilate pride and judgmentalism. Your prerequisite for reciprocal love must die, too. Are you willing to let go of these, once and for all? Will you become a channel and allow Christ's accepting love and forgiveness to flow through you?

If you're still inhaling and exhaling, it's not too late to start anew. Where you are. Right now.

Is there something you need to do—today?

Something you need to say—today?

For all you have is this day, this moment. Tomorrow may be too late.

Speak your love while ears can hear it. Write your love while eyes can read it. Through the Holy Spirit's enabling, you can be the woman of faith God intends you to be, the mother He would have you to be. Even if your relationship with your child is withered and stunted, He can bring forth verdant new life. Commit it to Him and trust Him.

This day, this minute, is the time to nourish the bond between you and your child. Little by little your nurturing, loving care will deepen the bond between you. One day true friendship will bloom to delight you and cheer you both through all your days.

On that day—if not before—your children will arise and call you blessed (Prov. 31:28). And you will praise your God, who gave you the privilege of motherhood!

## For Further Reading:

Buth, Lenore. *Empty Nest Parents.* (Christian Parent Series) Concordia, 1979. Emotions and relationships as parents enter this new phase of life; thought questions at end of each chapter.
Dobson, Dr. James C. *Straight Talk to Men and Their Wives.* Word Books, 1980. Practical advice on parenting and marriage that is useful to both

sexes; helpful in understanding differences between male and female points-of-view.

Erickson, Kenneth. *The Power of Praise.* Concordia, 1984. Stresses the importance of praise in interpersonal relationships; offers captivating examples and suggestions to help one become more affirming of others.

Landorf, Joyce. *Changepoints.* Revell, 1981. Good insights into the aspects and stages of a woman's life, including motherhood.

Swindoll, Charles R. *Home: Where Life Makes Up Its Mind . . .* Multnomah, 1979. Humorous, everyday illustrations from family life with Scriptural applications interwoven throughout.